PROVERBS 31

BITE SIZED BIBLE STUDIES

Satisfied Lives For Desperate Housewives

God's Word On Proverbs 31

6 SESSIONS

BETH JONES

When your words came, I ate them;
they were my joy and my heart's delight . . .
Jeremiah 15:16 NIV

The Bite Sized Bible Study Series Includes . . .

- Satisfied Lives For Desperate Housewives: God's Word On Proverbs 31
- Kissed or Dissed: God's Word For Feeling Rejected & Overlooked
- Grace For The Pace: God's Word For Stressed & Overloaded Lives
- Don't Factor Fear Here: God's Word For Overcoming Anxiety, Fear & Phobias
- The Friends God Sends: God's Word On Friendship & Chick Chat
- What To Do When You Feel Blue: God's Word For Depression & Discouragement

Beth Jones is a Bible teacher, author, wife and mother of four children who ministers the Word of God in a relevant and inspiring way by sharing down-to-earth insights. She is the author of the popular Bible study series *Getting A Grip On The Basis* which is being used by thousands of churches in America and abroad, *Why The Gory, Bloody Details?*, and the *Bite Sized Bible Study Series*. Beth also writes a bi-weekly newspaper column titled *"Just Us Girls"* and hosts www.bethjones.org. She and her husband Jeff founded and serve as the senior pastors of Kalamazoo Valley Family Church.

Beth Jones may be reached @
Kalamazoo Valley Family Church, 269.324.5599
www.bethjones.org or www.kvfc.org

PROVERBS 31

BITE SIZED BIBLE STUDIES

Satisfied Lives For Desperate Housewives

God's Word On Proverbs 31

6 SESSIONS

BETH JONES

ALLEY PRESS
PUBLISHERS

Valley Press Publishers

Portage, MI

valleypresspublishers.com

Satisfied Lives For Desperate Housewives
God's Word On Proverbs 31
ISBN: 1-933433-04-3

Copyright © 2005 Beth Ann Jones

Published by Valley Press Publishers - A Ministry of KVFC
995 Romence Road, Portage, MI 49024
800-596-0379   www.kvfc.org

Printed in the United States of America.
ALL RIGHTS RESERVED.

For information: Please contact Valley Press Publishers.

Contents

Acknowledgments

Writing a book is like having a baby! I've been "pregnant" with many books over the years and I've found that once a book is "conceived" by the Holy Spirit and begins to grow, the gestation period can range from a few years to several decades. Then, it seems that at the right time, when I'm "full-term" and "great with child", the Lord puts an "urge" to write within me which eventually triggers the labor pains, transition and ultimately the birth of a book! It takes a lot of people to give birth to a book and I'd like to honor those the Lord has put in my life to coach, pray, support and encourage me in these writing endeavors.

First, my husband, Jeff. You have been my best friend and most consistent encourager. When I have been uncertain, you've always been rock solid and gone the extra mile to help me fulfill God's will in writing. Thanks for loving me and believing in God's call on my life.

Second, my children, Meghan, Annie, Luke and Eric. I've had to take more time away to write; thanks for being understanding and willing to let mom go. I couldn't have asked for four better children. I love you all.

Third, my mom. What an inspiration you have always been to me! Thanks for letting me hang out with you in Florida to write these books.

Fourth, our staff. Our Associate Publisher, April Wedel, our Editorial Coordinator, Juli DeGraaf and our Publications Coordinator, Joanne Davis. I appreciate your love, faith, heart to get the Word out and the long hours you have spent helping me give birth to this book! I also want to thank the entire KVFC staff for their love, support and encouragement.

Fifth, all the volunteer copy editors and pray-ers. A very special thanks to Kim Sovine, Elise Burch and Missy Pluta for your time, comments and editing help. I especially appreciate my dear praying friends Mary VanderWal, Mary Jo Fox, Kate Cook, Cindy Boester, Colleen DeBruin, Jennifer Nederhoed, Pam Roe-Vanderberg, Jennifer Palthe, Molly Nicolai, KVFC prayer teams and many others who have continually lifted me and these projects to the Lord in prayer.

Sixth, Pat Judd, Bryan Norris and all the guys with CrossStaff. Thanks for partnering with us in this project. Let's have fun watching what the Lord will do!

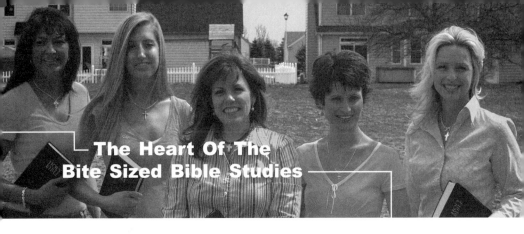

I love God's Word. I don't just like it; I love it. It's more valuable to me than anything. If I had to spend the rest of my life on a remote, uninhabited island and could only take one thing, I would take my Bible. Why? It's simple. God has changed and upgraded every area of my life as I have simply read, believed and obeyed the Bible.

It wasn't always that way. Like many people, I had never even considered reading the Bible for myself, much less studying it. The Bible was for priests, theologians and monks. It was not relevant to my life. It was a dusty old book in our basement. One day, when I was about 14 years old, I just got the "urge" to read the Bible. I started with Genesis, and within the first few chapters I fell asleep. That was the end of my Bible reading.

It wasn't until five years later when I was a 19-year-old college freshman that my roommate began to share with me what the Bible said about God, about life and about me. I was shocked at the "living" quality of the Bible. It wasn't like any other book I read. This wasn't like reading the president's biography. This wasn't like reading the dull Western Civilization textbooks in front of me. It was as if God Himself was explaining the contents to me. Something was happening in my heart as I read God's Word. I was challenged. I was encouraged. I was comforted. The Living God was speaking through His Living Word. During this time I developed a hunger for God and His Word. I stayed up late to read the Bible. I pondered it during the day. There was plenty I didn't understand, but I received strength, energy and wisdom just by reading it, and ultimately the Holy Spirit drew me to Jesus.

As a new Christian in my sophomore year of college, my Bible study leader simply exhorted me to read my Bible a lot and "let the Word of Christ dwell richly inside of me." It was the best advice ever! The result was that I began to develop an insatiable appetite for God's Word and a passionate desire to share God's Word with others. As I read my Bible, Jesus walked off the pages and came to live in my heart. Jesus isn't just alive in heaven, He is alive to me. I've come to know Him intimately through fellowship with Him in His Word.

Isn't it great that God's Word is interactive—not just historic or static? God's Word is living and active and able to effectually work within us to affect change and impart the miraculous! The Bible is the most amazing book ever! It has been banned, burned and blasted, but it lives on and continues to be the world's best-selling book.

Unfortunately, I have found that lots of people just don't understand the Bible and as a result, they get overwhelmed, bored or frustrated. Many Christians have never really tasted the rich, daily, life-changing flavor of God's Word. If you want to grow and mature in God, you have to "eat" large quantities of the Word. Once you taste and see that the Lord and His Word are good, nothing else will satisfy you! Think of it this way: if all you've ever tasted are peanut butter and jelly sandwiches, then you are pretty content with a good PBJ. But the minute you taste a filet mignon, you can never again be satisfied by a PBJ. In some ways, I have found that is the story for many Christians. If you're one of those people that have been content with a spiritual PBJ, I've got good news for you; get your taste buds ready for some rich, tasty, "meaty" morsels from God's Word. The more you eat it, the better it tastes!

Our goal in the Bite Sized Bible Study Series is to create an addiction in you for Bible study, and more importantly for knowing God intimately through the revelation knowledge of His Word, by His Spirit. As you explore these studies, I believe that the Holy Spirit will speak to your heart and transmit the supernatural revelation you need to operate victoriously in this life.

Jeremiah was right:

"When your words came, I ate them;
they were my joy and my heart's delight . . ."
Jeremiah 15:16, NIV

May this be your testimony, too!

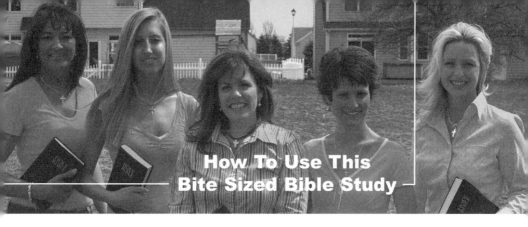

How To Use This Bite Sized Bible Study

This Bible study can be used individually as well as in small groups. It's ideal for those who are hungry to learn from the Word, but who have a limited amount of time to meet together with others.

The Bite Sized Bible Study Series is designed for all types of Bible study formats.

- Individual Study
- Women's Small Groups
- Lunchtime Study at Work
- Neighborhood Bible Study
- Couples' Small Groups
- Sunday School Class
- Prison Ministry
- Student and Youth Small Groups
- Outreach Bible Study
- Early Morning Men's Bible Groups
- Singles Small Groups
- Recovery and Felt Need Groups

For Individual Study

Pray. Ask God, by the Holy Spirit, to customize these sessions for you personally.

Expect. Turn your "expectation" on and trust God to speak to your heart.

Dive. Grab your Bible, pen and favorite beverage and dive in!

For Small Group Study Leaders

Pray. Ask God, by the Holy Spirit, to reveal and customize these sessions for you and your group members.

Expect. Turn your "expectation" on and trust God to speak to your heart, as well as the hearts of those in your small group.

Facilitate. Small groups will do better with a facilitator, preferably a more mature Christian who can add helpful comments as well as lead a heartfelt time of prayer before and after each session. It's important that you keep things moving in the right direction. As the leader of the small group, keep in mind that it's your job to facilitate discussion and not act as the "teacher" who does all the talking. It's important for those in the group to verbalize their discoveries, so do your best to create an atmosphere where each member feels free to share what they are learning from God's Word.

Encourage. Encourage everyone to participate. Help those who talk a lot to take a breather and let others share their insights as well.

Focus. Stay focused on God the Father, Jesus, and the Holy Spirit Who gave us the Scriptures. Our goal is to see what God has said in His Word. Keep in mind that this is a Bible study and not a place for "my opinion" or "my church believes" or "here's what I think" comments. Always direct people's attention back to the Bible to see what the Scriptures say.

Highlight. Hit the high points. If you face time constraints, you may not have enough time to cover every detail of each lesson. As the leader, prayerfully prepare and be sure you cover the highlights of each session.

Digest. We've endeavored to "cut up" the Word through this Bite Sized Bible Study, and as a leader it's your job to help those in your small group digest the Scriptures so they can benefit from all the spiritual nutrition in each word.

Discuss. Take time to answer the three discussion questions at the end of each Bible study session. These should help stimulate heartfelt conversation.

If you want this Bible study to really impact your life, you must be certain of one major thing: you must be certain you are a Christian according to God's definition and instruction in the Bible. You must be certain that you are accepted by God; that you are saved. So let's begin our study by considering this important issue.

Did you know that some people want to be a Christian on their terms, rather than on God's terms? Sometimes people want to emphasize church, religion and their goodness as evidence of their Christianity. For some, it will be a rude awakening to discover that the Bible tells us God isn't impressed by any of those substitutes. Did you know that God isn't interested in our denominational tags? He's not wowed by our church membership pedigree, either. He's not moved by our good deeds and benevolent accomplishments. The thing that most impresses God is His Son, Jesus Christ. *"For God so loved the world that he gave his one and only Son, that whoever believes in him shall not perish but have eternal life."* *John 3:16, NIV* God paid quite a price to send His own Son to the cross to pay the penalty for our sin. It's really an insult to Him to trust in or substitute any thing or anyone else for Jesus Christ. The key to being a Christian is to believe in, trust in, receive and confess Jesus Christ as your Lord and Savior.

Why would you or anyone want to believe in, trust, receive and confess Jesus Christ as Lord? Why would you want to know Jesus personally and to be known by Him? Unless you truly understand your condition before God, you wouldn't have any reason to! However, when you realize the magnitude of your sin—those private and public thoughts, deeds, actions and words that you and God know about—when you listen to your conscience and realize that truly "all have sinned," including you, it can be very sobering. It's even more sobering to realize that according to God's justice system, *". . . the wages of sin is death . . ."* *Romans 6:23 NKJV*. It's a big wake up call when it really hits you that the consequence of sin is death. Death which is defined as an eternal separation from God is the payment you will receive for your sin. When you realize your true, hopeless, lost condition before God, you will run to Him in order to be saved. This reality causes people to quit playing religious games and to quit trusting in their own works of righteousness. Our lost condition forces us to forgo being "churchy" or "religious", apathetic, passive and indifferent, and to become hungry for the Merciful Living God. It's good news to discover that *" . . . the gift of God is eternal life in Christ Jesus our Lord." Romans 6:23 NKJV*

What does God require of us? The qualification for eternal life is simply to believe on Jesus. Many people say they believe in God or in Jesus Christ. In fact, the Bible tells us that the devil himself believes and trembles. According to the Bible, God's definition of a Christian believer—or a Christ One—is the person who believes in their heart that God raised Jesus from the dead and who confesses with his or her mouth that Jesus Christ is their Lord. In other words, their heart and mouth agree that Jesus is Lord! We see this in Romans 10:13, 9, *". . . who-ever calls on the name of the LORD shall be saved . . . if you confess with your mouth the Lord Jesus and believe in your heart that God has raised Him from the dead, you will be saved." NKJV*

This is something we do on purpose. It's a sobering thought to consider that if you've never purposely repented of your sin and invited Jesus Christ to be the Lord of your life, you may not be saved—you may not be a Christian according to God's definition. Would you like to be certain that you are a Christian; that you have a relationship with the Lord and eternal salvation? It's simple, just answer these questions: Do you believe that God raised Jesus from the dead? Will you give Him the steering wheel of your life and trust Him to forgive all your sins and make you an entirely new person? Will you trust Jesus Christ alone to save you? Are you willing to invite Him into your life and will you confess that He is your Lord? If so, please pray this prayer from your heart. God will hear you, Jesus Christ will forgive your sins and enter your life. You will be a Christian.

"Dear God, I come to you as a person who recognizes my condition before you. I see that I am a sinner in need of a Savior. Jesus, I do believe that God raised You from the dead and I now invite you into my life. I confess Jesus as my Lord. I want to know You and be the Christian You have called me to be, according to Your definition. I thank You, in Jesus' Name. Amen."

This *Satisfied Lives For Desperate Housewives* Bible study is written for women, wives and moms of all ages, stages and seasons.

I love to see God work in the lives of women. I believe God is raising up a generation of on-fire, hip, Jesus-loving gals that are genuinely devoted to the Lord and who will influence their world for Christ!

I'd like to share a few thoughts with you before we launch into this study. I realize that there are women in all types of situations and circumstances and it's my prayer that something in each lesson will challenge you, encourage you and inspire you to be the gorgeous woman God has called you to be.

If you are *married*, I hope you will find many practical connecting points throughout this study.

If you are a *mom*, I trust you will be stirred up and helped in your important role as you study the lesson.

If you are *single, divorced or widowed,* I believe you, too, will glean important truths in each lesson. If you desire to be married, I hope the session on marriage will help you to prepare for your future.

If you *don't have children or if you've lost a child through death*, I pray that you are comforted and perhaps moved to pray for the children in your community or church as you look at the session on raising godly kids.

If you're a *teen, a Gen-X'er, a Buster, a Boomer, a Golden Gen or a Geezer,* I am believing God that this study will help lead you to a satisfied life in Jesus Christ. Let's get started—are you desperate for God, for balance, for a great marriage, for godly kids, for serving and for discovering your purpose?

Enjoy!

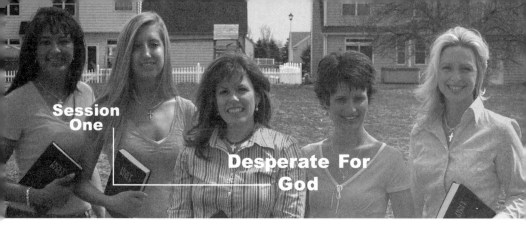

Desperate For God

The TV show *Desperate Housewives* is the rage. The ratings have soared as millions of people tune in each week. According to most recent descriptions, *Desperate Housewives* is a dark, racy, smash hit portraying the apparent domestic bliss of a group of wives—immoral tramps, bitter spies, out of control mothers and highly medicated women—in upmarket suburbia. "Housewives" is set on picture-perfect Wisteria Lane—one of the houses on the set was the home of Ward and June Cleaver (is that a bit ironic?).

USA Today reports the show averages 22.8 million viewers a week, and is the second-most-popular show on TV after CBS's *CSI*, according to Nielsen Media Research. The show is the favorite of 18 to 34-year-old viewers, as well as women 18 to 49 years old. The viewership is more upscale than usual, boasting more viewers with a college education and a household income of more than $75,000.[1]

How Desperate?

Is *Desperate Housewives'* unabashed immorality, gossip, sleaze and lust "normal" for the unfulfilled suburban wife? Does the show shock us? Should it? Does it entertain us? Are we desensitized and just "whatever" about it? Some people consider it a far-fetched spoof on suburbia, while others are living vicariously through it. It's not just women that flock to watch it, men are equally addicted. Christians, Pastors, Oprah and even the First Lady have made comments about the hit TV show. How desperate is the average housewife these days? What is she really desperate for? We've given pastoral care to enough married couples over the years to know that *Desperate*

There are only three types of people; those who have found God and serve him; those who have not found God and seek him, and those who live not seeking, or finding him. The first are rational and happy; the second unhappy and rational, and the third foolish and unhappy.
Blaise Pascal

Housewives is not far-fetched drama, but real life for many unsatisfied girls in society.

I think I am one of three people who have not seen an episode of *Desperate Housewives*. Not that I am the morality police, but I can't, in good conscience, watch the show. I'm not trying to throw stones, but I read in the Bible where it says something like, *"I will be careful to live a blameless life—when will you come to my aid? I will lead a life of integrity in my own home. I will refuse to look at anything vile and vulgar. I hate all crooked dealings; I will have nothing to do with them. I will reject perverse ideas and stay away from every evil. I will not tolerate people who slander their neighbors. I will not endure conceit and pride." Psalm 101:2-5, NLT*

I realize that our society has become so desensitized to immorality that many people are like, *"Whaaaat? Is there something wrong with it?"* I understand that God deals with all of us individually according to His Word, and each of us needs to be guided by our own conscience when it comes to what we watch, listen to and view. I am sure that someone could criticize us for watching *24, 20/20,* or *Fox News* with all the terrorism, violence and societal bizarreness on those programs. So, I am not throwing stones; just raising the subject.

The issue really isn't about *Desperate Housewives*, the question is: what nerve has this show hit? People *are* desperate, but are they finding satisfaction in the wrong things? People have an itch, but are they scratching the wrong spot? A lot of people are desperate these days; for fulfillment, for adventure, for relationships, for satisfaction and for success in every arena. It's as if *(hello?)* there really is a God-shaped vacuum or void on the inside of us! The Christian artists Plumb sang, *"There's a God-shaped hole in all of us and the restless soul is searching . . ."* Blaise Pascal, the French mathematician and physicist said, *"There is a God-shaped vacuum in the heart of every person and it can never be filled by any created thing. It can only be filled by God, made known through Jesus Christ."* It's true. Unfortunately, many people are desperately filling that void with substitutes.

Substitutes

I know some of the nicest women, wives and moms. They would do anything for you. They are great moms, school volunteers, friendly and just plain nice people, at the same time the God-shaped vacuum on the inside of their heart is not filled and many of them live in fear, anxiety, anger, jealousy, worry about their children and the fear of death. It breaks my heart to see them continually putting the square peg in the round hole of their hearts. They are "almost" fulfilled, but not genuinely.

Seeking, unbelieving, irreligious desperate housewives often seek to fill the God-shaped void in a variety of ways: if it's not in having a fling with John, the gardener, the UPS man or her best friend's man, she seeks to be satisfied and valued by golfing at the country club, volunteering for the Junior League, hooking up with this committee or that project, eating at the hip restaurants, redecorating her house, sending Johnny to a private school and private lessons, wearing her designer clothes, drinking another martini, eating anti-anxiety pills, dancing to the beat of the local rock band or jazzercise class, driving her Lexus, feeding her addictions, covering her compulsions, floating her boat, taking the European trip, being waxed, whitened, massaged, exfoliated, polished, cut and colored. The bottom line is that while many of these things are not necessarily bad, they do not provide satisfaction and are just counterfeits for the real McCoy. These seeking, unbelieving and irreligious women are desperately unfulfilled.

Sadly, even believing, true-blue Christian chicks often do something similar— they seek fulfillment and value in substitutes for God Himself through the lives of their children, their husband's success, their own careers, their church, friends and hobbies. They get busy and distracted in their social lives, their commitments and even at times doing what seem to be "Christian things," but they are not satisfied either. They are desperate.

The fake can never be the real. Desperation can never be satisfied with fake reality. Substitutes just don't cut it! A desperate housewife needs something real. I'm going to make a confession. I have knowingly purchased fake designer purses. It's true, don't stone me. I have never owned a "real" Louis Vuitton or Burberry purse. It was a temptation and I blew it! We were in New York City and although we never made it to Canal Street, there are plenty of vendors on every other street selling the fake-dog purses. These vendors put their obviously fake looking Kate Spade, Louis Vuitton, Coach and Burberry purses on the table which were sad looking imitations; not worthy of my cash.

However, I learned a little trick. If you know the correct lingo you can ask the vendor if he has any "other" purses for sale. I asked one fellow, *"Do you have any Louis Vuitton purses with the LV on them, or any other Burberry?"* He looked me over with his steely eyes and then he looked at my 6-foot-6, shaved-headed, goateed husband to determine if we were undercover police or NYC tourists. He decided he could trust us and I watched him walk over to the beat up van parked nearby. After shuffling around the van for a few minutes, he returned with several very nice, realistic-looking options for me to choose from. I bought three—two for me and one for a friend! When we walked away, I didn't know how to feel. On one hand I was thrilled that we had gotten a good deal on these fake purses; on the other hand I wondered if we had just done something illegal for which I needed to repent.

As I've shared this story with some girlfriends, we've had a few laughs over these fake purses. *And that's the point: they are fakes.* I know they are fakes. Everyone knows they are fakes. I advertise that they are fakes and I'm not trying to pretend they are real. *The question is: how many people are living a really fake life—and they know it's a big fake!—but they try to pretend that it's real?* Their life is a black hole, but they try to make everyone think they've got it all together.

The good news is that I *have* good news. God knew all this! He understands how we are wired and He knows what we need—real life in Him! The bottom line is this: *Desperate housewives need to get desperate for God.*

☙**Nugget**❧ Sorry to tell you that whether you're a believer or a die-hard agnostic or atheist, neither your success, your husband, your affairs, your kids, your wealth, your house, your addictions nor your stuff will ever fulfill you. Never. Have you figured that out yet? Fight it if you want to, but God has structured our existence in such a way that He is the only One that will truly, rock-bottom, heartfelt for real, satisfy us. Want to know why? News flash! Because Jesus is the cake and everything else is the frosting! Whenever we try to make anything else the cake and sprinkle God in here and there as the frosting, we miss it. It's backwards. Let's get it right.

The Proverbs 31 Woman Knows God

There is one gal that got it right! The Bible actually gives us an example of a woman with a high "get it" factor. A lot of people don't get it, but this chick does! Her name? The Proverbs 31 Woman. She gets it. She is the ideal Christian gal. She's got it together. She loves God. She's a great wife, her kids love her, she's successful in business enterprises and ministry, she's a good friend, she dresses to the nines, she's fun, wise, hip and got it going on. The best thing about her is that everything about her life stems from her walk with God. In this Bite Sized Bible Study we are going to get to know this gal and believe God that her traits will rub off on us!

I don't know about you, but before I really gave my life to Jesus Christ and got to know Him personally, I had a stereotypical idea of "Christian chicks." I thought to be a Christian you had to be some dull, vanilla, boring Jesus freak! I thought giving my life to Jesus 100% meant that I had to throw away my make-up, carry a big honkin' Bible, wear long skirts and turtleneck sweaters and sing hymns. I was not interested. At the time, I didn't know any on-fire, groovy Christian girls, but I believe God has been raising up a generation of sold-out, fired-up, hip and happening Christian women with genuine hearts after God, a pure and authentic life, their own sense of style, fashion and beauty, and women living purpose-filled lives! Are you one of those chicks? Would you like to be?

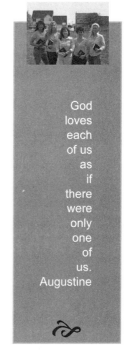

God loves each of us as if there were only one of us.
Augustine

There's a popular song called "Breathe" that describes the heart of a person desperate for God, and it depicts the Proverbs 31 woman.

This is the air I breath.
Your daily Presence.
This is my daily bread.

Your very Word spoken to me.
And I am desperate for You.
I'm lost without You.

Does this describe your heart's desire? Are you ready to get desperate for God and be on your way to becoming the Proverbs 31 woman God has called you to be? Let's begin our study in Proverbs 31 by reading the entire passage to get an overview of this lady.

The Proverbs 31 Woman

Who can find a virtuous and capable wife?
She is worth more than precious rubies.
Her husband can trust her,
and she will greatly enrich his life.
She will not hinder him but help him all her life.
She finds wool and flax and busily spins it.
She is like a merchant's ship; she brings her food from afar.
She gets up before dawn to prepare breakfast for her household
and plan the day's work for her servant girls.
She goes out to inspect a field and buys it;
with her earnings she plants a vineyard.
She is energetic and strong, a hard worker.
She watches for bargains; her lights burn late into the night.
Her hands are busy spinning thread, her fingers twisting fiber.
She extends a helping hand to the poor and opens her arms to the needy.
She has no fear of winter for her household
because all of them have warm clothes.
She quilts her own bedspreads.
She dresses like royalty in gowns of finest cloth.
Her husband is well known,
for he sits in the council meeting with the other civic leaders.
She makes belted linen garments and sashes to sell to the merchants.
She is clothed with strength and dignity,
and she laughs with no fear of the future.
When she speaks, her words are wise,

and kindness is the rule when she gives instructions.
She carefully watches all that goes on in her household
and does not have to bear the consequences of laziness.
Her children stand and bless her.
Her husband praises her:
"There are many virtuous and capable women in the world,
but you surpass them all!"
Charm is deceptive, and beauty does not last;
but a woman who fears the LORD will be greatly praised.
Reward her for all she has done.
Let her deeds publicly declare her praise.

Proverbs 31:10-31, NLT

Let's start our study of this Proverbs 31 woman by looking at her heart, desperate for God.

1.   Proverbs 31:30

Underline the phrase "worshipfully fears the Lord."

Charm and grace are deceptive, and beauty is vain [because it is not lasting], but a woman who reverently and worshipfully fears the Lord, she shall be praised! AMP

Listen to the New King James Version . . .

Charm is deceitful and beauty is passing, but a woman who fears the LORD, she shall be praised. NKJV

What does this verse tell us about this woman's relationship with God?

_____

_____

What does it mean to "fear the Lord"?

_____

_____

How do you describe "charm"? _____

Why is it deceitful? _____

Why is beauty vain or passing? _____

What does the woman who "fears the Lord" receive? _____

It's interesting that in the entire Proverbs 31 passage, this is the only verse that talks about this woman's relationship with the Lord. It's obvious that her walk with God splashes over into every other area of her life.

Let's talk about what it means to "fear the Lord." Does it mean we are to be afraid of God? According to the Bible God is love, so while we are to fear Him in the sense of reverence, respect and the fear of displeasing Him, we are not to be afraid of Him in the sense of dread or terror.

2.   1 John 4:16, 18-19

       Underline the words "love/loved" and "fear/fears."

       16 God is love. Whoever lives in love lives in God, and God in him . . . 18 There is no fear in love. But perfect love drives out fear, because fear has to do with punishment. The one who fears is not made perfect in love. 19 We love because he first loved us. NIV

       How does verse 16 describe God? _____

       Is there any fear in love? _____

What does perfect love do? _____

Why do we love God? _____

Describe your experience with "fearing God." _____

_____

Are you afraid of Him? _____

God wants us to have a healthy "fear of the Lord" based on the reality that He first loved us and we love Him back. Our hearts don't want to displease or disobey Him, but rather we want to know Him, walk with Him and please Him.

The Fear Of The Lord

The fear of the Lord is a subject that doesn't get talked about much. God doesn't want us to be afraid of Him in a negative sense, but a healthy respect and "fear" of God will cause His goodness to overflow into our lives. Let's look at the blessings promised to those who walk in the "fear of the Lord."

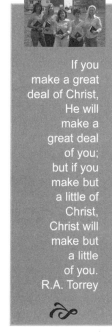

> If you make a great deal of Christ, He will make a great deal of you; but if you make but a little of Christ, Christ will make but a little of you.
> R.A. Torrey

1.   Psalm 25:12-14

      Underline the phrases "fears the Lord" and "fear him."

      12 Who, then, is the man that fears the LORD? He will instruct him in the way chosen for him. 13 He will spend his days in prosperity, and his descendants will inherit the land. 14 The LORD confides in those who fear him; he makes his covenant known to them. NIV

What five blessings are given to those who fear the Lord?

_____

_____

_____

_____

_____

Which of these five blessings do you desire the most at this time? Why?

_____

_____

_____

2.   Psalm 112:1-3

Underline the phrase "fears the Lord."

1 Blessed is the man who fears the LORD, who finds great delight in his commands. 2 His children will be mighty in the land; the generation of the upright will be blessed. 3 Wealth and riches are in his house, and his righteousness endures forever. NIV

If we fear the Lord, how will we feel about His Word or commands? _____

_____

This is huge! If we fear the Lord as the Proverbs 31 woman does, we will love God's Word. We will feed on, believe in and do His Word. I believe it's impossible to fear the Lord without absolutely delighting in His Word.

How would you describe your own hunger for God's Word at this time?

_____

What four blessings follow those who fear the Lord?

_____

_____

_____

_____

Which of these four blessings do you desire the most at this time, and why?

_____

3. Psalm 115:13-15

    Underline the phrase "fear the Lord."

    13 He will bless them that fear the LORD, both small and great. 14 The LORD shall increase you more and more, you and your children. 15 Ye are blessed of the LORD which made heaven and earth. KJV

    What does God promise to the families of those who fear the Lord? _____

    _____

4. Psalm 128:1-4

    Underline the phrases "fear the Lord" and "fears the Lord."

    1 Blessed are all who fear the LORD, who walk in his ways. 2 You will eat the fruit of your labor; blessings and prosperity will be yours. 3 Your wife will be like a fruitful vine within your house; your sons will be like olive shoots around your table. 4 Thus is the man blessed who fears the LORD. NIV

If we fear the Lord, what will we do with His ways? _____

Again, if we truly fear the Lord as the Proverbs 31 woman, we will not only fear God and love His Word, but we'll be obedient to do it. As we all know, it's not those who "talk the talk" that impress God, it's those who "walk the walk." When we live a life worthy of the Lord and fully pleasing to Him, we qualify for His amazing blessings.

What five blessings are promised to the person who fears the Lord?

_____

_____

_____

_____

_____

Which of these five blessings do you desire the most at this time, and why?

_____

5.   Deuteronomy 6:2-15

Underline the phrase "fear the Lord."

2 . . . so that you, your children and their children after them may fear the LORD your God as long as you live by keeping all his decrees and commands that I give you, and so that you may enjoy long life. 3 Hear,

O Israel, and be careful to obey so that it may go well with you and that you may increase greatly in a land flowing with milk and honey, just as the LORD, the God of your fathers, promised you. 4 Hear, O Israel: The LORD our God, the LORD is one. 5 Love the LORD your God with all your heart and with all your soul and with all your strength. 6 These commandments that I give you today are to be upon your hearts. 7 Impress them on your children. Talk about them when you sit at home and when you walk along the road, when you lie down and when you get up. 8 Tie them as symbols on your hands and bind them on your foreheads. 9 Write them on the doorframes of your houses and on your gates. 10 When the LORD your God brings you into the land he swore to your fathers, to Abraham, Isaac and Jacob, to give you—a land with large, flourishing cities you did not build, 11 houses filled with all kinds of good things you did not provide, wells you did not dig, and vineyards and olive groves you did not plant—then when you eat and are satisfied, 12 be careful that you do not forget the LORD, who brought you out of Egypt, out of the land of slavery. 13 Fear the LORD your God, serve him only and take your oaths in his name. 14 Do not follow other gods, the gods of the peoples around you . . . NIV

Write down all the things we are commanded to do.

_____

_____

_____

_____

_____

If we do these things and walk in the light of God's Word, what does He promise us?

_____

There is not an inch of any sphere of life over which Jesus Christ does not say, 'Mine.' Abraham Kuyper

_____

_____

Get the idea? Fearing God is a good thing. Take a moment and review the verses above, paying special attention to the way God offers to bless entire families—husbands, wives, children, homes and possessions—when we fear Him and give His Word first place in our lives.

Do you feel that you walk in the "fear of the Lord"? _____

In what ways can you improve and change in this area? _____

_____

_____

_____

Hunger And Thirst For God

We just hit the high points regarding the blessings of God for those who will walk in the fear of the Lord. God is so good and He's good all the time. When He makes a promise, if we fulfill the conditions He has laid down, we can be certain that He will make good on His Word!

Perhaps you are wondering how this can be more real to you. I want to share something that has helped me in my own personal walk with God and I trust that it will help you cultivate a lifestyle of living a life pleasing to the Lord and walking in the fear of the Lord in a healthy way. It's simply this: _get hungry and thirsty for God!_

Are you hungry or thirsty for God? How hungry or thirsty are you? It's simple to determine. A preacher friend of mine once said you can tell how hungry or how thirsty you are by asking this simple question: _"What does it take to satisfy me?"_ In other words, how much of God does it take to satisfy your heart? Do you need a lot of God? His Word? His Presence? Worship? Or will a little dab do ya? If you read your Bible once a month, attend church occasionally and pray every now and then, you are not very hungry and it doesn't take much of God to satisfy you. But if you are the person who can't get enough, then you are one hungry chick!

❧**Nugget**❧ Think about being hungry and thirsty for God as it relates to being hungry for food and thirsty for water. If you are really hungry for food—starving, famished, hungry with a capital H—would you be satisfied if I gave you a saltine cracker? No, you would not. It would take more than a saltine to satisfy your hunger. If you're really hungry, you want a Thanksgiving Feast! If you're thirsty for water—parched and cotton-mouthed—then would you be satisfied if I gave you a teaspoon of water? No! If you are thirsty, you need buckets of water to quench your thirst.

It's the same way with being hungry and thirsty for God. If you are really hungry for God—if you are craving and starving for Him—then would you be satisfied with reading your Bible ten minutes a week? Going to church once every other month? No way! If you are thirsty for God, will you be satisfied by singing a few worship songs every six months? Praying a few times a year? Absolutely not. If you are hungry and thirsty, it's going to take lots of time with the Lord in His Word, in prayer, in worship and in church to satisfy your appetite. The sad reality for many people is that they are not hungry for God, and one little spiritual saltine cracker is all it takes to satisfy them and one teaspoon of water nearly chokes them. If you want to know the truth, we have an epidemic of *"spiritually anorexic"* Christians walking around! (But, we'll save that topic for another book!) How hungry and thirsty are you?

Spiritual Hunger And Thirst Test

Be honest. Check out your spiritual hunger and thirst level by answering these questions:

	Yes	No
I read my Bible regularly.	❏	❏
I rarely read my Bible.	❏	❏
I go to church every week and feel energized.	❏	❏

	Yes	No
I go to church less than once a month and if the church service goes over one hour, I get antsy.	❑	❑
I look forward to our worship time and in my heart I wish we could sing and worship longer.	❑	❑
I do not enjoy the musical worship time and if we sing more than 3 songs, I get bored.	❑	❑
I pray all the time and never have enough time to pray about everything in my heart.	❑	❑
I get bored in prayer, run out of things to say and really only pray when there is an emergency.	❑	❑
I listen to Christian worship music on a regular basis.	❑	❑
I listen to mostly secular, pop or country music.	❑	❑
I read Christian books and magazines to feed my heart.	❑	❑
I read mostly secular books, novels and magazines.	❑	❑
I watch many movies, TV shows and DVDs that contradict my faith in God.	❑	❑
I try to limit my movie and TV viewing and DVD choices to things that are congruent with my faith in God.	❑	❑
I attend a Bible study or small group for spiritual growth on a regular basis.	❑	❑
I am hit or miss in my attendance of Bible study or small groups.	❑	❑

I think you can figure out what your answers mean. Perhaps it will help you to see your answers and make the necessary adjustments.

If you are hungry for God, it will take a lot of God to satisfy your appetite. The more time you spend with the Lord in honest, heartfelt conversation and in listening to Him as you read the Bible, the hungrier and thirstier you will get. Don't go on a "God-fast," eat more and more of His reality in your life! The way to stir up hunger and thirst is to eat and drink more!

There was a woman in the Bible who found out how thirsty for Jesus she was. She's known as the woman at the well. Read this passage and pay attention to words like "drink," "food," "water" and "thirsty."

Soon a Samaritan woman came to draw water, and Jesus said to her, "Please give me a drink." He was alone at the time because his disciples had gone into the village to buy some food. The woman was surprised, for Jews refuse to have anything to do with Samaritans. She said to Jesus, "You are a Jew, and I am a Samaritan woman. Why are you asking me for a drink?" Jesus replied, "If you only knew the gift God has for you and who I am, you would ask me, and I would give you living water." "But sir, you don't have a rope or a bucket," she said, "and this is a very deep well. Where would you get this living water? And besides, are you greater than our ancestor Jacob who gave us this well? How can you offer better water than he and his sons and his cattle enjoyed?" Jesus replied, "People soon become thirsty again after drinking this water. But the water I give them takes away thirst altogether. It becomes a perpetual spring within them, giving them eternal life." "Please, sir," the woman said, "give me some of that water! Then I'll never be thirsty again, and I won't have to come here to haul water. John 4:6-15, NLT

When we have Jesus, He satisfies our thirst. Let's look at this.

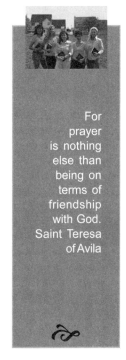

For prayer is nothing else than being on terms of friendship with God.
Saint Teresa of Avila

1. Matthew 5:6

   Underline the words "hunger" and "thirst."

   Blessed are those who hunger and thirst for righteousness, for they shall be filled. NKJV

   Who does God promise to fill? _____

   In your own words, describe hunger and thirst. _____

   _____

   _____

   I love the way The Message translation of the Bible puts this verse:

   You're blessed when you've worked up a good appetite for God. He's food and drink in the best meal you'll ever eat.

2. Psalm 63:1-5

   Underline every word that references the act of eating or drinking.

   God—you're my God! I can't get enough of you! I've worked up such hunger and thirst for God, traveling across dry and weary deserts. 2 So here I am in the place of worship, eyes open, drinking in your strength and glory. 3 In your generous love I am really living at last! My lips brim praises like fountains. 4 I bless you every time I take a breath; My arms wave like banners of praise to you. 5 I eat my fill of prime rib and gravy; I smack my lips. It's time to shout praises! The Message

   Sometimes people are hungrier for His goodness rather than for Him.

   Who was the psalmist starving for—God or His blessings? _____

Notice how this person verbalized their hunger to God directly! If you were going to verbalize your own hunger for God, what would you say to Him?

_____

3.   Psalm 119:20

Underline every word that references the act of eating or drinking.

My soul is starved and hungry, ravenous!—insatiable for your nourishing commands. The Message

What is this person hungry for? _____

Describe your own hunger level for the Word and how you satisfy that hunger.

_____

4.   Psalm 119:40

Underline the phrase "how hungry I am."

See how hungry I am for your counsel . . .

What is this person hungry for? _____

≈**Nugget**≈ When you are at home or work and you find yourself hungry, what do you do? Generally, you get up and fix yourself something to eat, or you run up to the nearest restaurant or convenience store to grab a bite. You do something to satisfy your hunger. Have you ever noticed that being hungry alone doesn't satisfy your hunger? In other words, you could sit in the chair all day and say, *"I sure am hungry. Boy oh boy, am I hungry. I am just starving . . ."* But if you never get up from the chair and eat something, you'll continue to be hungry! It's the same way where spiritual hunger is concerned. If we are hungry for God, we have to get up and eat! Make your body read your Bible, pray and go to church on a regular basis. Just like you eat three meals a day, your spiritual life needs regular meals.

The Secret Is Seeking

Have you noticed that God has never obligated Himself to be found by the casual, lazy, half-hearted and apathetic seeker? But God has promised that we would find Him if we seek Him with our whole heart. Let's look at this.

1.   Jeremiah 29:13-14

Underline the words "seek" and "search."

13 And you will seek Me and find Me, when you search for Me with all your heart. 14 I will be found by you, says the LORD . . . NKJV

If we want to find God, what are we required to do? _____

Describe the intensity with which we are to seek. _____

Do you think that God will be found by those who are half-hearted, lukewarm, lazy, apathetic, que sera, sera?

_____

Listen to the way The Message translation conveys this passage:

13 'When you come looking for me, you'll find me. Yes, when you get serious about finding me and want it more than anything else, 14 I'll make sure you won't be disappointed.' GOD's Decree.

Do you get the idea? God is not impressed by "pretend" seeking. But He does promise that when we get serious about finding Him more than anything else, we will find Him and be satisfied.

Are you ready to get your heart into seeking God? _____

In your own life, how do you seek God on a regular basis? _____

_____

⊱Nugget⊰ He is looking for those who seek Him with their whole heart! That means that you jump in with both feet. You are not living on the fence or trying to be the "churchy" girl on Sundays and the "worldly" girl the rest of the week. He's looking for gals whose lives are congruent and are whole hearted for Him!

2.   Psalm 105:4

Underline the word "seek."

Seek, inquire of and for the Lord, and crave Him and His strength (His might and inflexibility to temptation); seek and require His face and His presence [continually] evermore. AMP

What 3 words does this passage use to describe the idea of "seek"? Here's a hint . . .

I_____

C_____

R_____

What does it mean to "inquire"? _____

_____

What does it mean to "crave"? _____

_____

⊱

What does it mean to "require"? _____

_____

3.   Psalm 22:26

Underline the words "seek," "eat" and "satisfied."

The poor and afflicted shall eat and be satisfied; they shall praise the Lord—they who [diligently] seek for, inquire of and for Him, and require Him [as their greatest need]. May your hearts be quickened now and forever! AMP

Who will eat and be satisfied? _____

What is their greatest need? _____

4.   Psalm 27:8

Underline the word "seek."

You have said, Seek My face [inquire for and require My presence as your vital need]. My heart says to You, Your face (Your presence), Lord, will I seek, inquire for, and require [of necessity and on the authority of Your Word]. AMP

What did the Lord say? _____

What does our heart say to the Lord? _____

What does it mean to you to "require My presence as your vital need"?

_____

What does the phrase "require of necessity" mean to you? _____

_____

I have found that in my own life as the pace, pressure, deadlines and the responsibility of raising four children, writing and helping my husband pastor a growing church increases, I need more of God's Presence in my life. I can't make it on my own. I am not that smart. I don't have that much energy. I know what it's like to be desperate for God; to seek, crave and require Him and to find Him! I don't want to imagine life any other way.

How about you? I am sure you want to be a good Christian, a great wife, mom and fruitful for God in whatever you do, and I trust you've been stirred up and reminded that the life you want starts with the fear of the Lord and your own hunger and thirst for God through Jesus Christ. Charm and favor are deceitful and beauty is vain and vanishing, but the woman who fears the Lord shall be praised—blessed and satisfied!

Is your heart stirred up? Are you desperate for God? Have you located your own spiritual hunger and thirst levels and are you ready to make a change? Is it time for you to seek God with your whole heart, no holding back, no being lukewarm, but 100% in pursuit of God? I believe that there are four types of girls doing this lesson.

#1: Seeker Sally

Perhaps you realize that you really don't know God. You've never established a real personal relationship with Jesus Christ. It starts when you humble yourself, repent of your sins and simply invite Jesus into your life to be your Lord and Savior. Are you ready to invite Jesus to be the Lord of your life? Are you ready to have Him forgive you of every one of your sins? Give you a new start in life? Have eternal life? If so, let's pray:

"Dear God, I come to you and I recognize my condition before you. I see that I am a sinner in need of a Savior. I seek You. I am desperate for You. Jesus, I believe that God raised You from the dead, and I invite You into my life to be my Lord and Savior. Help me to be the woman you have called me to be. Amen."

#2: Lukewarm Linda

Perhaps you realize that you've really been a "lukewarm" Christian. You're not on fire for God, but you don't hate the Lord, either. Jesus had some harsh words for the half-hearted, luke-warm believers, *"I know all the things you do, that you are neither hot nor cold. I wish you were one or the other! But since you are like lukewarm water, I will spit you out of my mouth!"* Revelation 3:15-17, NLT Are you ready to repent? Change? Get hot? Hungry? Desperate? Let's pray:

"Dear Father, I repent for being so stinkin' lukewarm. I want to be hungry and thirsty for You. I surrender my life to You and I ask You to revive me according to Your Word; light the fire in me Lord. I choose to seek You, I am desperate for You and I ask You to surround me with people who will help me to be the on-fire Christian woman You have called me to be. In Jesus' Name. Amen."

#3: Backslidden Betty

Maybe you realize that you've lost your first love. You've backslid in your walk with God and allowed the cares of this life, the deceitfulness of riches, busyness and the love of other things and what others think of you to choke God and His Word right out of your life. Are you ready to get it right? Ready to repent and return to your first love? Jesus said this, *"But I have this [one charge to make] against you: that you have left (abandoned) the love that you had at first [you have deserted Me, your first love]. Remember then from what heights you have fallen. Repent (change the inner man to meet God's will) and do the works you did previously [when first you knew the Lord], or else I will visit you and remove your lampstand from its place, unless you change your mind and repent."* Revelation 2:4-5, AMP It's time to return to the things you did in your walk with God in the very beginning—remember? Read your Bible. Pray. Go to church. Get to know Him again! Let's pray:

"Dear Father, I repent for backsliding and moving away from my first love. I have let other things creep in and steal Your place in my life. Jesus, You are my first love and I want to rekindle our relationship and do the things I did when I first knew You. I am asking You to help me to pray, seek You and knit my heart to You in a new and fresh way. Thank You for Your forgiveness and for restoring me as I return to You. Help me to be the Christian woman you have called me to be. In Jesus' Name. Amen."

#4: Hungry Helen

If your heart is stirred up, fired up and ready to know God in a greater way, it's time to seek Him like never before. Let's pray:

"Dear Father, You are my all in all. I am so hungry for You. I thirst for Your Presence, Lord. I seek You with my whole heart and I crave and require You as the necessity in my life. Speak to me through Your Word and by Your Spirit. Help me to live a life worthy of You and fully pleasing to You in every way. I choose to walk in the fear of the Lord and I trust You to make me the woman You have created me to be. In Jesus' Name. Amen."

Scriptures To Chew On

Taking time to meditate on and memorize God's Word is invaluable. Hiding His Word in our hearts will strengthen us for the present and arm us for the future. Here are two verses to memorize and chew on this week. Write these verses on index cards and carry them with you this week. If you will post them in your bathroom, dashboard, desk, locker or other convenient places, you will find these Scriptures taking root in your heart.

> *"Desperate, I throw myself on you:*
> *you are my God!"*
> *Psalm 31:14, The Message*

> *"When I was desperate, I called out,*
> *and GOD got me out of a tight spot."*
> *Psalm 34:6, The Message*

Group Discussion

1.   Describe the profile of the type of Christian woman you want to be.

2.   Describe the biggest challenges and hindrances to your own spiritual walk with God.

3.   Describe some proactive steps you are going to take to pursue being hungry and thirsty for God on a regular basis.

[1]http://www.usatoday.com/money/media/2004-12-12-desperate-usat_x.htm

Desperate For Balance

How do you spin all the plates? How do you juggle every ball thrown at you? Is it possible to keep up with the Joneses? Be Supermom? Find balance? With more of us women in the workforce and raising families at the same time, how does a girl do it all? The sad reality is that many women aren't able to do it all! Most women are out of balance in one way or another—workaholics, mom-aholics, obbessive-compulsaholics, hobby-aholics, exercise-aholics, alcoholics, spendaholics—you name an addiction and some mom has it. Is it really possible to find balance in life, marriage, parenting and work? Without God, no! With God, yes—if you'll follow His Word.

The Proverbs 31 Woman is balanced. She's real. She has a great personality. She laughs, she's a "get er done" type of girl, she has street smarts, she adores her family, she has a sweet spirit, she's very influential **and** she loves God. She's got it going on. She's an inspiration. What we don't see is some "he-woman" who wears the pants in the family; we don't see a mousy, doormat, hyper-submissive woman who's afraid of her own shadow; we don't see a stuffy, churchy, religious persona; and yet, we don't see a carnal, sleazy, flesh-dominated, addictive, sensual woman either. She's godly and she's balanced. I love that.

God's not looking for Christian clones or carbon-copy church chicks. He's looking for women that are surrendered to Him in every way and who will allow Him to emboss His thumbprint in their lives and very personalities! As I mentioned in Session 1, I've always believed it was possible to be a genuine, on-fire, Bible-thumping, Spirit-filled,

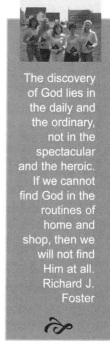

The discovery of God lies in the daily and the ordinary, not in the spectacular and the heroic. If we cannot find God in the routines of home and shop, then we will not find Him at all.
Richard J. Foster

gospel-preaching, hip Christian chick who loves the Lord and lives to please Him while influencing the world around her. The Proverbs 31 Woman did this and so can you and I!

What Are You Worth?

Finding balance starts with seeing ourselves the way God does. The first verse of the Proverbs 31 Woman passage starts like this: *"A capable, intelligent, and virtuous woman—who is he who can find her? She is far more precious than jewels and her value is far above rubies or pearls."* AMP The writer wasn't kidding—who can find a girl like this? Godly, balanced, strong, wise, motivated and productive. She's a rare find, for sure.

As we begin our study, let's talk about a general truth this verse brings up: our value! In God's eyes, we are already highly valued as His daughters. In fact, when we were sinners, God loved us enough to send Jesus to our rescue! Jesus paid the highest price to purchase us, and it's important that we rest in the fact that He already values us highly! Our worth in His sight is far above rubies.

⮞**Nugget**⮜ What is the value of something? The value of something is determined by the price someone will pay for it. So, what's your price? You are more valuable than you realize. Have you priced a ruby lately? I have. According to a local jeweler, you could spend as much as $25,000 for a one carat ruby! Well, your value is *far above* rubies—that's rubies, plural. You are not equated with some sliver of a cubic zirc—no, your value is far above rubies.

Your value has been determined by the price Someone was willing to pay for you. Obviously, God thinks your worth is more than rubies as He sent His Son, Jesus Christ, to pay quite a price for you. He bought you with His own blood. Let's not insult God by thinking less of ourselves than He does! Okay?!

Ten Personality Traits Of The Balanced Woman

With that said, let's begin our study on being *Desperate For Balance* by looking at some highlight verses in Proverbs 31 and discovering *"Ten Personality Traits of the Balanced Woman."*

#1 Trait: Spiritual Strength

1.   Proverbs 31:17

Underline the words that depict spiritual strength.

She girds herself with strength [spiritual, mental, and physical fitness for her God-given task] and makes her arms strong and firm . . . AMP

In what areas did this woman make herself strong? _____

Why did she need to be strong? _____

There is no way that you or I could be like the Proverbs 31 woman without spiritual strength—which is the result of a strong walk with God.

This woman was "on purpose" about it. She "gird" herself, which simply means to "put on like a belt." She expected and actively put on spiritual strength, which led to mental strength and physical fitness.

2.   Proverbs 31:29

Underline the words that depict spiritual strength.

Many daughters have done virtuously, nobly, and well [with the strength of character that is steadfast in goodness], but you excel them all . . . AMP

How does this woman stack up in life? _____

What exceeding traits does this woman have? _____

_____

To be consistently strong in character and goodness (i.e., honesty, faithfulness, integrity, ethics, generosity, discretion, etc.) requires a strong connection with God—a real relationship that is cultivated on a regular basis.

How do you cultivate this type of relationship with God? _____

_____

#2 Trait: Led By The Spirit

In this day and age, we have got to know how to hear from God. We must be led by the Spirit and be in the right place at the right time, making the right choices and hooking up with the right people. We can't do this on our own, but if we are led by the Spirit, He'll lead us into God's best.

1.   Proverbs 31:15

Underline the time of day that she goes to get spiritual food.

She rises while it is yet night and gets [spiritual] food for her household and assigns her maids their tasks. AMP

How do you think this woman gets "spiritual food" for her household?

_____

It sounds like she has her own personal quiet time with God for prayer, fellowship and hearing from Him on behalf of her family and her responsibilities.

Do you have a daily quiet time with God where you can get the spiritual food, direction and assignments for the day? If so, describe it.

_____

_____

2.   John 16:13

Underline all the pronouns of the Holy Spirit (He, His).

However, when He, the Spirit of truth, has come, He will guide you into all truth; for He will not speak on His own authority, but whatever He hears He will speak; and He will tell you things to come. NKJV

What will the Holy Spirit do for us? _____

Can we expect the Holy Spirit to guide us and show us things to come regarding our lives and the lives of those in our family?

_____

≈**Nugget**≈ Did you know that often the Holy Spirit will let you know things about your children, your husband and your own life before they happen? For instance, let's say you have one child who is hanging with the wrong crowd or surfing inappropriate sites on the Internet. If you stay sensitive to God, in prayer and in seeking Him and listening to the Holy Spirit, He will often tip you off or He will supernaturally show or impress upon you things you otherwise would not know.

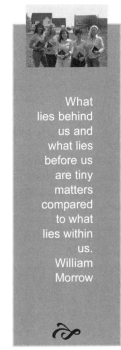

What lies behind us and what lies before us are tiny matters compared to what lies within us.
William Morrow

3.   Romans 8:14-15

Underline the word that describes what the Spirit of God does for us.

For as many as are led by the Spirit of God, these are sons of God. NKJV

If we are children of God, who's supposed to be leading us? _____

_____

It's a great comfort to know that you don't have to be a woman, wife, mom all by yourself! The Holy Spirit lives inside of us and He promises to lead us. Let's purpose in our hearts that we will be sensitive and listen to His direction.

#3 Trait: Organized Manager

1.   Proverbs 31:14-15, 19

Underline all the verbs.

31:14-15 She is like the merchant ships loaded with foodstuffs; she brings her household's food from a far [country] . . . She rises while it is yet night and gets [spiritual] food for her household and assigns her maids their tasks. AMP

Underline the phrase "home and hearth."

31:19 *She's skilled in the crafts of home and hearth, diligent in homemaking. The Message*

What does this lady provide for her family? _____

This lady knows how to shop at Sam's Club! She's a good shopper and likely finds good deals, too.

Do you get the idea? She is making the oversight, management and organization of her home a priority. How many of us have room for improvement? And all the sisters said, Amen!

To whom does she assign tasks? _____

In order to assign tasks, what must you be? _____

Organized! As a wife and mom, you already know how quickly things can become chaotic at home. Organization may not be your strength, but all of us can and should manage and administrate the sphere of our home. When possible, things like shopping, cleaning, cooking, laundry and basic chores can be scheduled, assigned and maintained on a regular basis.

What are your strengths in crafts, decorating, cooking and homemaking?

_____

2.   Proverbs 31:27

Underline the phrase "She looks."

She looks well to how things go in her household, and the bread of idleness (gossip, discontent, and self-pity) she will not eat. AMP

What is her responsibility at home? _____

What does she stay away from? _____

How would you define a modern woman who feeds on gossip, discontent and self-pity?

_____

3.   Proverbs 31:25

Underline every word that describes the Proverbs 31 woman.

Strength and dignity are her clothing and her position is strong and secure; she rejoices over the future [the latter day or time to come, knowing that she and her family are in readiness for it]! AMP

This woman has a nice disposition. How does she feel about the future?

_____

What does she know about her family that allows her to laugh? _____

_____

She has managed her home and the lives of her children enough to know that things are organized, prepared and ready. She appears to be the type of person that has made the proper deposits into her husband, her children and domestic arenas so regardless what the future holds, they are ready.

Is your family ready for the future so you can rejoice as you look ahead?

_____

Most families today think about things like the mental, emotional, spiritual and physical health of our children—did we prepare them properly? College funds, retirement funds, health insurance, investments—have we prepared our finances sufficiently for the future? Often husbands and wives will work together to be certain these things are ready. Then they can rejoice both in the present and as they look ahead. Time is ticking, are you prepared?

4.   1 Timothy 5:14

Underline the phrase "manage their homes."

So I counsel younger widows to marry, to have children, to manage their homes and to give the enemy no opportunity for slander. NIV

Describe what it means to manage your home. _____

_____

What planning system, tools, calendars, schedules, etc. do you employ?

_____

5. Titus 2:3-5

Underline the phrase "to be busy at home."

3 Likewise, teach the older women to be reverent in the way they live, not to be slanderers or addicted to much wine, but to teach what is good. 4 Then they can train the younger women to love their husbands and children, 5 to be self-controlled and pure, to be busy at home, to be kind, and to be subject to their husbands, so that no one will malign the word of God. NIV

What is the role of older women? _____

_____

What is the role of younger women? _____

_____

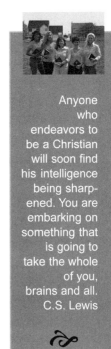

In the New Testament culture, women were primarily stay-at-home wives and mothers. Today, many women must work outside the home and they face challenges with balancing their home life, family life and work life.

Anyone who endeavors to be a Christian will soon find his intelligence being sharpened. You are embarking on something that is going to take the whole of you, brains and all.
C.S. Lewis

If you work outside the home, have you and your spouse discussed sharing the household duties or perhaps hiring some domestic help?

If so, what plan have you come up with?

_____

#4 Trait: Mentally Sharp

1.   Proverbs 31:17

Underline the word "mental."

She girds herself with strength [spiritual, mental, and physical fitness for her God-given task] and makes her arms strong and firm . . . AMP

How do you think she girds herself with mental strength? _____

_____

What do you do to stay mentally sharp, educated, informed? _____

_____

❧**Nugget**❧ Have you considered any of these options? Furthering your education? Learning computer skills? Taking a college course or community education class to expand your knowledge base? We should never stop learning and growing. Even such simple things as crossword puzzles, chess and computer games that stimulate our thinking processes are good mental exercises. Stay sharp mentally. You can do it!

2.   Romans 12:2

Underline the phrase "renewing of your mind."

Do not conform any longer to the pattern of this world, but be transformed by the renewing of your mind. Then you will be able to test and approve what God's will is-his good, pleasing and perfect will. NIV

What does God want our minds to be renewed or reprogrammed to? _____

_____

•**Nugget**• The best way to develop a sharp mind and maintain peace of mind is to keep your mind full of God and His Word. When He fills our thoughts there isn't any room for anxiety, worry, fear, depression or other negative ways of thinking.

#5 Trait: Physically Fit

Being physically fit is important for women of all ages. Proper weight, healthy blood pressure, strong bones and muscle mass will keep you strong and fit for serving God and enjoying life with your family.

1.   Proverbs 31:17

Underline the phrase "physical fitness."

She girds herself with strength [spiritual, mental, and physical fitness for her God-given task] and makes her arms strong and firm . . . AMP

How do you think she girds herself with physical strength? _____

_____

What do you do to stay physically fit? _____

_____

2.   Proverbs 23:2

Underline the word "gluttony."

. . . and put a knife to your throat if you are given to gluttony. NIV

If you have food issues—gluttony—what are you supposed to do? _____

_____

≈Nugget≈ Lots of women are plagued by weight problems and the health challenges they cause. As you know, there are all kinds of books, systems and programs designed to help people lose weight. I encourage you to seek the help and support you need to lose the weight you'd like to shed. Find a friend and work together to get to your desired weight and size.

Describe your strategy for the implementation of eating nutritious foods.

_____

3.   1 Timothy 4:8-9

Underline the phrase "workouts in the gymnasium."

8 Workouts in the gymnasium are useful, but a disciplined life in God is far more so, making you fit both today and forever. 9 You can count on this. Take it to heart. The Message

What do workouts in the gym do for us? _____

What does a disciplined life in God do for us? _____

4.   1 Corinthians 6:19-20

Underline the phrase "place of the Holy Spirit."

19 Or didn't you realize that your body is a sacred place, the place of the Holy Spirit? Don't you see that you can't live however you please, squandering what God paid such a high price for? The physical part of you is not some piece of property belonging to the spiritual part of you. 20 God owns the whole works. So let people see God in and through your body. The Message

Who owns your body? _____

Who should be seen in your body? _____

This is challenging, isn't it? Jesus purchased us and our bodies with His blood. The Holy Spirit lives inside our bodies, so let's give Him a home that reflects God's glory.

#6 Trait: Full Of Faith

1.   Proverbs 31:21

Underline the phrase "fears not."

She fears not the snow for her family, for all her household are doubly clothed in scarlet. AMP

I love this passage.

What does this woman not allow herself to do?

_____

Do you live in fear and worry regarding your family?

_____

Little faith will bring your soul to heaven, but great faith will bring heaven to your soul.
Charles H. Spurgeon

❧**Nugget**❧ As a person who's lived in Michigan the majority of my life, I am acquainted with snow! I've seen plenty of accidents over my lifetime and have experienced a few slips and slides going 65 miles an hour on the freeway. I know what it's like to pray and believe God for His protection at the beginning of the winter season. I know that our family is covered in "scarlet": the blood of Jesus. Often, my husband and I will verbalize our faith in God by praying a prayer like this over ourselves and our children: *"We thank You Father that our entire family is protected and covered in the blood of Jesus, covered by the Name of Jesus and surrounded by the angels of God. You protect us and watch our going out and coming in."* We believe that He does and this removes fear.

2.   Hebrews 11:1

Underline the things faith perceives.

Now faith is the assurance (the confirmation, the title deed) of the things [we] hope for, being the proof of things [we] do not see and the conviction of their reality [faith perceiving as real fact what is not revealed to the senses]. AMP

What is faith, according to this passage? _____

_____

What does faith perceive? _____

3.   Hebrews 11:6

Underline the words "faith," "please God," "rewards" and "seek him."

And without faith it is impossible to please God, because anyone who comes to him must believe that he exists and that he rewards those who earnestly seek him. NIV

What is it impossible to do without faith? _____

Why do you think this is true? _____

What does God promise for those who earnestly seek Him? _____

_____

#7 Trait: Joyful

The Proverbs 31 woman is one happy chick! I love the fact that she rejoices and laughs. Laughter and joy need to be a regular part of our lives!

1.   Proverbs 31:25

Underline the phrase "she can laugh."

She is clothed with strength and dignity; she can laugh at the days to come. NIV

What does this woman do regarding the future? _____

When you think about the world, the present and the future, are you worried, fearful, depressed and anxious, or laughing?

_____

What enables a person to laugh at the future? _____

2.   Ecclesiastes 3:1-8

Underline the words "season," "purpose" and "time."

1 To every thing there is a season, and a time to every purpose under the heaven: 2 A time to be born, and a time to die; a time to plant, and a time to pluck up that which is planted; 3 A time to kill, and a time to heal; a time to break down, and a time to build up; 4 A time to weep, and a time to laugh; a time to mourn, and a time to dance; 5 A time to cast away stones, and a time to gather stones together; a time to embrace, and a time to refrain from embracing; 6 A time to get, and a time to lose; a time to keep, and a time to cast away; 7 A time to rend, and a time to sew; a time to keep silence, and a time to speak; 8 A time to love, and a time to hate; a time of war, and a time of peace. KJV

This is a great, classic passage on a season for everything.

What does verse 4 tell us? _____

Is it time for you to laugh? _____

What makes you laugh? _____

3.   Philippians 4:4

Underline the phrase "full of joy."

Always be full of joy in the Lord. I say it again—rejoice! NLT

How often are we to be full of joy? _____

How do you define "full"? _____

Would those close to you describe you as a joyful person with an easy laugh?

_____

Take a moment to itemize the things you can be full of joy about. _____

_____

_____

#8 Trait: Speaks Wisely

1.   Proverbs 31:26

Underline the words "mouth" and "tongue."

*She opens her mouth in skillful and godly Wisdom, and on her tongue
is the law of kindness [giving counsel and instruction]. AMP*

When this Proverbs 31 lady opens her mouth, people listen.

What type of wisdom does she give? _____

In what way or with what tone does she give wisdom? _____

Someone has said that the difference between knowledge and wisdom is
this: knowledge knows what and wisdom knows what to do about it.

2.   Proverbs 2:6

Underline the phrase "the Lord gives wisdom."

*For the LORD gives wisdom, and from his
mouth come knowledge and understanding. NIV*

Who gives wisdom?

_____

If you find yourself struggling in life as the result of
making unwise choices or if you'd like to increase
in wisdom, spend extra time reading the book of
Proverbs. It is loaded with God's wisdom.

Be
kind,
for
everyone
you
meet
is
fighting
a
hard
battle.
Plato

#9 Trait: Kindness

1.   Proverbs 31:26

Underline the phrase "the law of kindness."

She opens her mouth with wisdom, and on her tongue is the law of kindness. NKJV

What law does this woman live by? _____

As a wise woman, we want to speak in a way that people can receive what we are sharing. Whether we are relating to our husband, kids or friends, if the "law of kindness" is in our tongues then we won't come across with harsh, critical, condescending, patronizing, whiney or pouty tones. Right?

2.   Proverbs 16:24

Underline the phrase "kind words."

Kind words are like honey—sweet to the soul and healthy for the body. NLT

What do kind words do? _____

_____

Describe the last time someone spoke these kinds of words to you?

_____

3.   Galatians 5:22-23

Underline the phrase "fruit of the Spirit."

22 But the fruit of the Spirit is love, joy, peace, patience, kindness, goodness, faithfulness, 23 gentleness and self-control. Against such things there is no law. NIV

There is no law against kindness! You'll never be arrested for kindness or any of these fruits. List the 9 fruits of the Spirit:

_____ _____ _____

_____ _____ _____

_____ _____ _____

#10 Trait: Productive And Fruitful

1.   Proverbs 31:31

Underline the words "give her," "the fruit" and "works praise her."

Give her of the fruit of her hands, and let her own works praise her in the gates [of the city]! AMP

What do we eventually reap? _____

God has established the law of sowing and reaping. It's a law that works, regardless of the seeds we plant. If you spend your life planting good seeds into the lives of your family and others, you will reap a rich harvest. If you plant bad, negative, hurtful seeds into the lives of your family and others, you will reap heartache and pain. If you choose not to plant, but through apathy and laziness you don't plant any seeds at all, you will likely reap a famine.

We can see that this woman reaped the fruit of her hands—in her family, in her business and in her influence in the city. A balanced harvest from a balanced life!

2.   Galatians 6:7-10

Underline the words "sows" and "reaps."

7 Do not be deceived: God cannot be mocked. A man reaps what he sows. 8 The one who sows to please his sinful nature, from that nature will reap destruction; the one who sows to please the Spirit, from the Spirit will reap eternal life. 9 Let us not become weary in doing good, for at the proper time we will reap a harvest if we do not give up. NIV

What do we reap? _____

If we sow "bad" seeds, what will we reap? _____

If we sow "godly" seeds, what will we reap? _____

Why are we encouraged not to get weary? _____

Have you ever been weary? I think we've all felt the frustration of patiently waiting for the harvest! We sow and sow and sow, and at times it looks like those seeds are not producing anything good. But be encouraged by God's Word that as we sow and stay patient, we will reap!

Balance. We all want it, and if we will focus on the *Ten Personality Traits Of The Balanced Woman,* we'll find it.

Scriptures To Chew On

Taking time to meditate on and memorize God's Word is invaluable. Hiding His Word in our hearts will strengthen us for the present and arm us for the future. Here are two verses to memorize and chew on this week. Write these verses on index cards and carry them with you this week. If you will post them in your bathroom, dashboard, desk, locker or other convenient places, you will find these Scriptures taking root in your heart.

"And the Child grew and became strong in spirit,
filled with wisdom; and the grace of God was upon Him."
Luke 2:40, NKJV

"But grow in the grace and knowledge of our Lord and Savior Jesus Christ.
To him be glory both now and forever! Amen."
2 Peter 3:18, NIV

Group Discussion

1.   Describe all the plates you are required to spin and the balls you must juggle. What are your biggest challenges and successes?

2.   Describe your general sense of self-worth. Have you struggled to see your value in God's eyes, or has it been easy for you to recognize how valuable you are to Him?

3.   Look over the Ten Personality Traits of the Balanced Woman and describe the two that you most need to improve.

Personal Notes

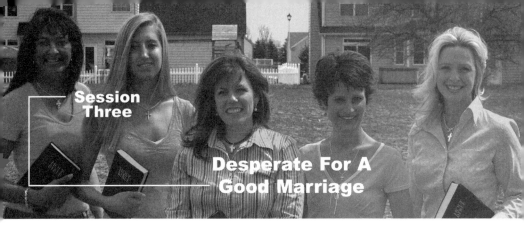

The story goes that a woman died and went to heaven. When she got to the Pearly Gates she asked St. Peter how to get into heaven. Peter said, *"It's simple, just spell one word."* *"Great,"* she replied, *"what's the word?"* Peter answered, *"Spell L-O-V-E."* The woman proceeded to spell L-O-V-E perfectly and St. Peter welcomed her into heaven. After a few moments, Peter asked the woman to guard the Pearly Gates as he had to run an errand. She asked him, *"What should I do if someone shows up at the Gates?"* St. Peter replied, *"You'll know what to do."* Peter left and within a few minutes this woman's husband showed up at the Pearly Gates. *"What are you doing here?"* the woman asked him. *"I don't know,"* the man answered, *"I must have died and now here I am at the Pearly Gates. How do I get in?"* *"It's easy,"* she responded, *"you just have to spell one word."* *"Really?"* he said, *"What's the word?"* *"Czechoslovakia"* she answered! (In case you wondered, this is not how you get into heaven!)

Doesn't sound like a happy marriage, does it? God wants happy marriages! Marriage is God's idea. It was the first institution He created. He blessed it. He wants it to work. Really, God wants us to have an awesome marriage, but as you know, everyone doesn't have a marriage made in heaven; rather they are enduring a marriage that is hell on Earth!

God's Word outlines the secret to walking in His blessings as a husband and wife. If you want to do marriage your way or the world's way, plan on hell on Earth. The selfish nature of each person cannot be overcome and eventually the "love" will be gone, anger and resentment will set in,

A good marriage is the union of two forgivers.
Ruth Bell Graham

and distance and coldness will dominate a marriage. If you want to do it God's way, He'll help you make the adjustments, love with His love and enjoy a marriage made in heaven.

Fortunately, for most of our married life, my husband and I have enjoyed a marriage made in heaven. We've had our bumps, like any marriage does, but we can honestly say that because Jesus Christ is the Lord of our individual lives and the Lord of our marriage, we've experienced God's blessings in our relationship. It has not been easy. We've had to make a lot of decisions to put one another first and not ourselves. We've had to communicate, work it out and forgive. We've been mad. We've had words. We've had pity parties. In the end, we've chosen to love and forgive and God just continues to knit our hearts together. I recently told my husband, while we were on a cruise in the Bahamas (without children!) that I am really looking forward to our empty-nest years because we have so much fun together. I mean it, and that is a God-thing. I know everyone doesn't have this type of story, but in time and with God's help, you can.

&**Nugget**&. Often there are women who found Christ after they were married and since their husband is not a believer, they have to deal with lots of issues; or there are some women who are much more interested in the things of God than their husbands and this creates its own set of problems. Sometimes, the husband is on fire for the Lord and the wife acts like the wet blanket; this is not God's best for either party. It's challenging and requires God's wisdom, and thank God He's willing to help us!

Then there are other stories straight from *Desperate Housewives*—stories of adultery, orgies, chat room affairs and all kinds of bizarre activity. Broken-hearted wives are all around us and it's very possible this type of pain is being experienced by someone in your neighborhood! If you are the wife who's reeling from the reality of your husband's unfaithfulness, and you're not even sure you can forgive, trust again or want it to work; you need answers and godly counsel. I encourage you to talk with your pastor or Christian counselor to get the input you need for your specific situation. I am believing God that this Bible study will help to encourage you as well.

Maybe you're the one who's had an affair, cheated on your husband and now your marriage is barely hanging on by a thread. You need help in the form of godly repentance, God's forgiveness, accountability, godly counsel and strength to make right choices if your marriage is to have any chance of survival.

❧**Nugget**❧ You have to fight for your marriage. We live in an age where sensuality, premarital sex, adultery, divorce and every variation of sexual preference is in our face 24/7. You and your husband cannot escape the sexual onslaught that targets you everyday via television, DVDs, movies, commercials, grocery checkout counter magazines, billboards, e-mail and the Internet. If you want the type of marriage God has planned for you and your spouse, you will have to stand against every temptation thrown at you from this tidal wave of immorality. It's possible, and for the health of your marriage and family, you must take a stand to enjoy the marriage God wants for you and your spouse.

Let's look at some realities that you'll probably never see on *Desperate Housewives*. God's Word warns us about the pain of immorality.

Desperate Housewife Realities

Hollywood makes adultery, immorality and free sex look appealing, exciting and without consequences. On a recent TV talk show, one of the guests that had committed adultery suggested that 90% of married men have committed or entertained the idea of adultery. That is a sad speculation. The problem is that in real life, adultery and immorality create heartbreak and pain for all parties involved. Let's look at this.

1.   Proverbs 11:29

       Underline the phrase "bring trouble." Circle the phrase "inherit only the wind."

       Those who bring trouble on their families inherit only the wind . . .
       NLT

What reality will the person who brings trouble on their families through their selfish choices inherit?

_____

&**Nugget**&> I've seen this up close and personal. A husband or wife is in a season of frustration in their marriage and they make the bad choice to have an affair or walk away from their family. Their choice definitely troubles their family and without fail, in the end they inherit the wind. Often, as time goes on, they find that their relationships with the kids are empty, detached, full of strife, bitterness and obligatory love. They often have nothing but their gold chains, polyester shirts, convertible sports cars, fishing boats and other "toys" to show for their lives. They've inherited nothing!

2.   Proverbs 2:16-20

Underline the phrase "immoral woman."

16 Wisdom will save you from the immoral woman, from the flattery of the adulterous woman. 17 She has abandoned her husband and ignores the covenant she made before God. 18 Entering her house leads to death; it is the road to hell. 19 The man who visits her is doomed. He will never reach the paths of life. 20 Follow the steps of good men instead, and stay on the paths of the righteous. NLT

What saves you from the immoral person? _____

Describe the _modus operandi_ of the adulterer. _____

_____

What reality happens to the person who chooses the adultery path? _____

_____

3.   Proverbs 5:3-23

Underline the phrase "immoral woman."

3 The lips of an immoral woman are as sweet as honey, and her mouth is smoother than oil. 4 But the result is as bitter as poison, sharp as a double-edged sword. 5 Her feet go down to death; her steps lead straight to the grave. 6 For she does not care about the path to life. She staggers down a crooked trail and doesn't even realize where it leads. 7 So now, my sons, listen to me. Never stray from what I am about to say: 8 Run from her! Don't go near the door of her house! 9 If you do, you will lose your honor and hand over to merciless people everything you have achieved in life. 10 Strangers will obtain your wealth, and someone else will enjoy the fruit of your labor. 11 Afterward you will groan in anguish when disease consumes your body, 12 and you will say, "How I hated discipline! If only I had not demanded my own way! 13 Oh, why didn't I listen to my teachers? Why didn't I pay attention to those who gave me instruction? 14 I have come to the brink of utter ruin, and now I must face public disgrace." 15 Drink water from your own well—share your love only with your wife. 16 Why spill the water of your springs in public, having sex with just anyone? 17 You should reserve it for yourselves. Don't share it with strangers. 18 Let your wife be a fountain of blessing for you. Rejoice in the wife of your youth. 19 She is a loving doe, a graceful deer. Let her breasts satisfy you always. May you always be captivated by her love. 20 Why be captivated, my son, with an immoral woman, or embrace the breasts of an adulterous woman? 21 For the LORD sees clearly what a man does, examining every path he takes. 22 An evil man is held captive by his own sins; they are ropes that catch and hold him. 23 He will die for lack of self-control; he will be lost because of his incredible folly. NLT

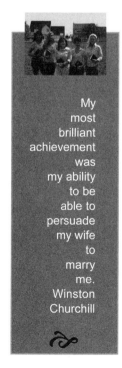

My most brilliant achievement was my ability to be able to persuade my wife to marry me.
Winston Churchill

This is a long passage that's worth reading several times. Here God shows us the way immoral people (both men and women) operate and the results of following these people.

What do verses 15-19 tell us about avoiding adulterous relationships and giving attention to our own spouse?

_____

_____

What realities do you glean from this passage regarding the destruction that accompanies those that find pleasure in affairs and adultery?

_____

_____

4.   Proverbs 7:6-27

Underline the phrase "immoral woman."

6 I was looking out the window of my house one day 7 and saw a simpleminded young man who lacked common sense. 8 He was crossing the street near the house of an immoral woman. He was strolling down the path by her house 9 at twilight, as the day was fading, as the dark of night set in. 10 The woman approached him, dressed seductively and sly of heart. 11 She was the brash, rebellious type who never stays at home. 12 She is often seen in the streets and markets, soliciting at every corner. 13 She threw her arms around him and kissed him, and with a brazen look she said, 14 "I've offered my sacrifices and just finished my vows. 15 It's you I was looking for! I came out to find you, and here you are! 16 My bed is spread with colored sheets of finest linen imported from Egypt. 17 I've perfumed my bed with myrrh, aloes, and cinnamon. 18 Come, let's drink our fill of love until morning. Let's enjoy each other's caresses, 19 for my husband is not home. He's away on a long trip. 20 He has taken a wallet full of money with him, and he won't return until later in the month." 21 So she seduced him with her pretty speech. With her flattery she enticed him. 22 He followed her at once, like an ox going to the slaughter or like a trapped stag, 23 awaiting the arrow that would pierce its heart. He was like a bird flying into a snare, little knowing it would cost him his life. 24 Listen to me, my sons, and pay attention to my words. 25 Don't let your hearts stray away toward her. Don't wander down her wayward path. 26 For she has been the ruin of many; numerous men have been her victims. 27 Her house is the road to the grave. Her bedroom is the den of death. NLT

This is another long passage that is worth reading several times, and like the previous Scripture, it shows us the way immoral people operate and the results of following them.

What realities do you glean from this passage regarding the lies and deception that accompanies those that find pleasure in affairs and adultery?

_____

You don't have to sign for the package of a dissatisfied marriage, adultery and sensual temptations that the devil delivers to your marriage every month. But, it's going to take work. It takes two to tango in marriage. In a perfect world both the husband and wife are surrendered to the Lordship of Jesus Christ, both are functioning in their God-given roles and walking in love. It makes it a lot easier, but it still takes work! It takes humility. It takes patience. It takes forgiveness.

A Marriage Of Three

Before we even begin to talk about the marriage relationship, let's talk about you as a woman and wife and your relationship with God. If you want your marriage to make it, it's going to require three of you!

↝**Nugget**↝ I was raised by a single mom and by God's grace she did a great job raising me and my three sisters. God's mercy reached down and He helped us, but I'm convinced from experience and from God's Word that the best scenario is when one man and one woman form a union with Jesus Christ at the center and they raise their children by God's design. The Bible has been saying that for years: *"Two are better than one, because they have a good reward for their labor. For if they fall, one will lift up his companion. But woe to him who is alone when he falls, for he has no one to help him up. Again, if two lie down together, they will keep warm; but how can one be warm alone? Though one may be overpowered by another, two can withstand him. And a threefold cord is not quickly broken." Ecclesiastes 4:9-12, NKJV*

Let me give you a little exercise that my husband and I heard years ago. We've shared this with couples over the years to put things into perspective.

A True Love Triangle

On your sheet of paper draw a triangle.

At the top point of the triangle put "Jesus."

At the bottom left of the triangle write your name.

*At the bottom right of the triangle write your husband's name
(fiancé's name, boyfriend's name or
if you're waiting for God's mate for you, write "to be announced.")*

*Now, draw an arrow on the outside of the triangle
that goes from your name up to Jesus.*

*Draw an arrow on the outside of the triangle
that goes from your husband's name up to Jesus.*

*If both individuals are focused on Jesus Christ
and growing in their relationship with Him,
notice what happens to the distance between*

the husband and the wife as each person gets closer to Jesus.

Notice the distance between the husband and wife
by looking at the bottom line of the triangle.

Now, draw 3 horizontal lines inside the triangle
that are parallel with the bottom line of the triangle.

Notice how each line gets smaller and smaller as you get closer to Jesus.
This represents the reality that the husband and wife get
closer and closer to one another as they purpose to get closer to Jesus.

Thus, a threefold cord is not easily broken! This is God's best: a marriage of three! The third Person in our marriage needs to be Jesus Christ. When He is allowed to take His place in our life and marriage, His plan goes into operation.

Let's look at three keys to being the wife you are called to be in a marriage of "three."

#1. Know That You Are Already Complete In Him

Sometimes single women will say, *"I feel so incomplete. I feel like half-a-person. I can't wait to meet my spouse so I will finally feel complete."* That is a faulty way to think. You are already complete—in Christ! It's important that you realize that, while your husband will be one of God's major blessings in life, you are already complete in Christ. *". . . you are complete in Him."* Colossians 2:10, NKJV Settle this once and for all in your heart: because of Jesus Christ you are a whole person—complete and lacking nothing.

Marriage is our last, best chance to grow up.
Joseph Barth

#2. Find Your Satisfaction In God Alone

Marriage is very satisfying, but it's not supposed to take the place of God in our lives. I picture it this way: at the head of the table of my heart, there is a seat reserved for One Person—Jesus Christ. I can't put my husband or any other person in that seat. Jesus sits at the Head of the table of my heart, and all the other chairs around that table are to be filled by my husband, children, family and friends the Lord brings into my life. Have you thought about it this way?

Jesus is the satisfier of our heart and whenever we try to find our satisfaction in anyone else, we will be let down. Other people, including our husband, are not designed to fill that role in our lives. When Jesus satisfies you, it frees you up to be a spout of blessing, rather than a sponge that needs something from others. The psalmist summarized it this way: *"For He satisfies the longing soul, and fills the hungry soul with goodness." Psalm 107:9, NKJV*

#3. Let God Meet All Of Your Expectations

If you want to take instant pressure off your marriage, transfer your expectation from your spouse to God. In other words, lower the bar on your husband and raise the bar on God. If you expect your husband to make you happy, you'll be disappointed. If you expect your husband to understand you, provide for you, meet all your needs, treat you like a queen and cater to your every whim—forget about it. You have set yourself up for a life of disappointment because your expectation is in the wrong place! Only God can truly fulfill our expectations. Expect God to make you happy, forgive you, understand you, provide for you, meet your needs and treat you like the royal daughter you are, and then if He chooses to use your husband to meet some of those things—great. However, He may choose to use other people or He may choose to work in your heart to rearrange your desires. When our expectation is in God, it frees up everyone around us. It removes disappointment from our lives, because if in a healthy way we don't expect things from people, they cannot disappoint us. (I realize that some people have taken this position based on hurts, resentment and pain, and unfortunately, they are living very bitter, disappointed lives.) Listen to what the Scriptures say: *"My soul, wait only upon God and silently submit to Him; for my hope and expectation are from Him. Psalm 62:5, AMP*

The Proverbs 31 Woman As A Wife

You can be sure that no matter what condition your marriage is in, there is only one person you can control and change. Guess who it's not? It's not your husband; you can't control him, although many wives try! The only person you can control and change is yourself, ladies. The only way to totally embrace God's plan for your marriage and make the choice to be a giver—focusing on your spouse's needs rather than your own—is to be secure and fulfilled in your own relationship with God. The Proverbs 31 woman knows something about her role and how to bring out the best in her husband and in their marriage. Let's begin.

She Does Him Good

1.   Proverbs 31:11-12

Underline the phrases "her husband trusts" and "She comforts, encourages, and does him only good . . ."

11 The heart of her husband trusts in her confidently and relies on and believes in her securely, so that he has no lack of [honest] gain or need of [dishonest] spoil. 12 She comforts, encourages, and does him only good as long as there is life within her. AMP

Trust is a huge issue in marriage. Jealousy, anger, rage, accusation and suspicion stem from a heart of distrust. Cultivating trust in marriage will bring a great deal of peace and tranquility.

Describe the heart of her husband. What three things is his heart able to do in relationship to his wife?

T_____

R_____

B_____

Why do you think these things are important in a marriage? _____

_____

Describe the role of trust in your marriage. _____

_____

The reason the heart of her husband can trust, rely and believe in her is because of the way she relates to him.

What three things does this wife do for her husband?

C_____

E_____

D_____

In what ways do you or could you comfort, encourage and do good to your husband?

_____

_____

Listen to the way a few other versions of the Bible translate verses 11 and 12.

The heart of her husband safely trusts her; so he will have no lack of gain. She does him good and not evil all the days of her life. NKJV

Her husband can trust her, and she will richly satisfy his needs. She will not hinder him but help him all her life. TLB

Let's look at that verse again in The Living Bible and talk about this phrase "richly satisfying his needs." *(I know, I can hear some of you screaming, "What about my needs???? It's always about his needs!!!" Just calm down, we'll get to your needs later.)* I love Dr. Laura's book, *The Proper Care and Feeding of Husbands*, in which she hits this topic with force.[1] According to numerous marriage experts, our husband's needs can be boiled down to these basics.

He Needs Affirmation And Admiration

1.   Ephesians 5:33

Underline the words "wife" and "she." Circle the words "husband" and "him."

> *. . . let the wife see that she respects and reverences her husband [that she notices him, regards him, honors him, prefers him, venerates, and esteems him; and that she defers to him, praises him, and loves and admires him exceedingly].* AMP

Yes, you know your husband has faults—so do you! Criticizing and finding fault is the easy part. The challenging part that goes against our human nature is to focus on our spouse's strengths.

What twelve words are listed to help us know how to relate to our husband?

_____   _____

_____   _____

_____   _____

_____   _____

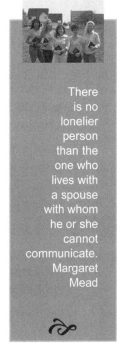

There is no lonelier person than the one who lives with a spouse with whom he or she cannot communicate.
Margaret Mead

_____   _____

_____   _____

Which of these is the easiest for you? _____

_____

Which of these is the hardest for you? _____

Write a 50-word "gush" describing the great traits of your husband: _____

_____

_____

_____

_____

_____

_____

What do you think about sharing this with your husband?

2.   1 Peter 3:1-2

Underline the words "married women," "wives," "she," "husbands" and
"him."

*1 In like manner, you married women, be submissive to your own
husbands [subordinate yourselves as being secondary to and
dependent on them, and adapt yourselves to them], so that even if any
do not obey the Word [of God], they may be won over not by
discussion but by the [godly] lives of their wives, 2 When they observe*

the pure and modest way in which you conduct yourselves, together with your reverence [for your husband; you are to feel for him all that reverence includes: to respect, defer to, revere him—to honor, esteem, appreciate, prize, and, in the human sense, to adore him, that is, to admire, praise, be devoted to, deeply love, and enjoy your husband].
AMP

This passage goes against our culture of male-bashing. I am all in favor of women being strong and independent, but at the same time God wants our marriages to be healthy, flowing with His structure and blessed.

How do you define submission according to this verse? _____

_____

If your husband is not a believer, what does this verse tell you will win him quicker than your preaching?

_____

How are we to respond to our husbands? _____

_____

He Needs A Fun Friend And Recreational Companion

1. Ecclesiastes 9:9

    Underline the phrase "live happily."

    Live happily with the woman you love through the fleeting days of life, for the wife God gives you is your best reward down here for all your earthly toil. TLB

    God wants husbands and wives happy!

What hobbies does your husband enjoy that you could share with him?

_____

My husband loves to ride his motorcycle and he likes me to be his passenger. When the weather is good, we make it a point to go for rides together. We'll find little cafés or back roads to visit and have a great time together. He wants and needs my companionship and these little trips have helped bond us together.

2.   Colossians 3:18

Underline the words "subject," "subordinate" and "adapt."

Wives, be subject to your husbands [subordinate and adapt yourselves to them], as is right and fitting and your proper duty in the Lord. AMP

What are we to do as wives? _____

_____

☞**Nugget**☜ Submission has become such a negative word in secular and Christian circles. *"I am woman, hear me roar"* has become the theme song for many woman. How about putting your "gun" down and looking for ways to enjoy life with your husband? You might be surprised to know that he'd like to spend more time with you, if you weren't whining or criticizing him. If your husband likes to fish, or watch football, or ride bikes, why don't you ask him if he'd like your company and enjoy these recreational hobbies together? What is his favorite meal? Restaurant? Activity? Surprise him and enjoy it together.

He Needs Sexual Fulfillment

Speaking of his favorite activity! Sex is a good thing. Sex is a God thing. He created us to enjoy sexual relations with our spouse. Reaching fulfillment in the sex act brings a great deal of unity, joy and peace to the marriage relationship.

Unfortunately, many Christian gals have been given an unhealthy view of sex with their husbands and they "endure" or dutifully perform sex with their husbands, rather than enjoying it. God wants us to enjoy sex as much as our husbands do!

You heard about the couple that went to the doctor, right? The doctor pulled the wife aside and told her, *"You're husband is going to die unless you do three things."* Willing to do anything to help her husband, she asked, *"What three things doctor?"* *"First, you'll have to wait on him hand and foot 24/7. Second, you'll have to compliment and admire him 24/7. Third, you'll have to have sex with him 24/7."* The woman went out to the waiting area where her husband was sitting and he asked her, *"What did the doctor say?"* She replied, *"You're gonna die."*

So, let's have a little sex talk! Remember, God wants you and your husband to be as free, "naked and unashamed," as Adam and Eve were in the garden before the fall!

1. Proverbs 5:18-20

    Underline the words "wife," "she" and "her."

    18 Let your wife be a fountain of blessing for you. Rejoice in the wife of your youth. 19 She is a loving doe, a graceful deer. Let her breasts satisfy you always. May you always be captivated by her love. 20 Why be captivated, my son, with an immoral woman, or embrace the breasts of an adulterous woman? NLT

    What does God want the sexual relationship to be like for you and your husband?

    _____

    Satisfaction! Are you both satisfied? Talk with your husband about what satisfies him in the bedroom

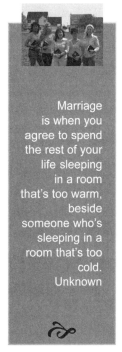

Marriage is when you agree to spend the rest of your life sleeping in a room that's too warm, beside someone who's sleeping in a room that's too cold.
Unknown

and share with him what satisfies you!

What is your body designed to give your husband?

_____

_____

Face it girls, your husband is turned on by looking at your body! Strange, isn't it? Our husband's don't understand why they can walk around the house naked and we can still read our magazine, unaffected! Men and women are just created differently. Women need more emotional and physical touch to get the passion going.

It seems unfair, doesn't it? He can be ready to go in a microsecond by just looking at you; while perhaps it takes you a bit longer to get in the groove. As someone has said, men are like microwaves and women are like crock pots.

Many women desire and enjoy the sexual relationship just as much as men do, but generally speaking our husband's are going to have a stronger sex drive than us gals, and it's important that we do our best to keep up! Be the one who satisfies your husband's God-given need for sexual intimacy.

2.   1 Corinthians 7:3-6

Underline the word "deprive."

3 The husband should not deprive his wife of sexual intimacy, which is her right as a married woman, nor should the wife deprive her husband. 4 The wife gives authority over her body to her husband, and the husband also gives authority over his body to his wife. 5 So do not deprive each other of sexual relations. The only exception to this rule would be the agreement of both husband and wife to refrain from sexual intimacy for a limited time, so they can give themselves more

completely to prayer. Afterward they should come together again so that Satan won't be able to tempt them because of their lack of self-control.
NLT

According to verses 3-5, what should you not deprive your husband of?

_____

Who has authority over your body? _____

3.   1 Corinthians 6:20

Underline the phrase "honor God."

. . . you were bought at a price. Therefore honor God with your body.
NIV

Do you think you could actually honor God by giving your body to your husband in sexual intimacy?

_____

It's true. You can honor God with your body by giving yourself to your husband.

4.   1 Samuel 16:7

Underline the phrases "man looks at the outward appearance," and "the Lord looks at the heart."

But the LORD said to Samuel, 'Do not look at his appearance or at his physical stature, because I have refused him. For the LORD does not see as man sees; for man looks at the outward appearance, but the LORD looks at the heart.' NKJV

What does the Lord look at? _____

What do men look at? _____

⊱**Nugget**⊰ So girls, whether we like it or not or whether it's right or not, it's a fact—men look on the outward appearance. It's great that the Lord looks on the heart, but it's a truth that people, especially men, look on the outer appearance. That means that you need to pay attention to your appearance: your weight, your clothing, your hair, your make-up and all that superficial stuff! Perhaps it's a bitter pill to swallow, but if your husband was honest, he'd like you to look nice, to dress in attractive attire and to keep your weight at a reasonable place.

Let's talk about clothing for a moment. We've all done it. *"Honey, does this outfit make me look fat?"* Then we turn around and ask him from every angle. What is he supposed to say? *"Yes, you look like Shamu."* Your man wants you to look good. The Proverbs 31 woman knows how to dress to the nines: *"She dresses like royalty in gowns of finest cloth."* *Proverbs 31:22, NLT* Is it possible to dress in a hip, modern, fashionable way and stay modest? These days the concept of modesty has often been forgotten. Let's get real girls: do we need to have plunging necklines? Bare midriffs? Fannies hanging out to be stylish? I am all for staying current with our fashion, just stay modest, too. The basic rule on modesty is that you don't dress in a way that causes other men to stumble, lust or become inflamed in passion. So ladies, you will have to make a choice on how low your shirts will be, how high your skirts will be, where your top will land in your midriff and how tight everything is. Some people believe that women should wear long skirts, long sleeves and zero makeup. That would actually scare my husband!

God is not against us dressing nicely, wearing jewelry or styling our hair, but He is interested in us focusing more on inner beauty and good deeds than outer beauty. As one old preacher used to say: *"If the barn needs painting, paint it."* That fits a lot of us women! I love how the New Living Bible describes dressing modestly, *"And I want women to be modest in their appearance. They should wear decent and appropriate clothing and not draw attention to themselves by the way they fix their hair or by wearing gold or pearls or expensive clothes. For women who claim to be devoted to God should make themselves attractive by the good things they do." 1 Timothy 2:9-10*

Okay, back to your husband's need for sex! In summary, maybe you have some questions or concerns regarding the sexual relationship with your husband. God's best is that the sexual relationship is mutually satisfying and that both partners are comfortable with the sex act. It's important to communicate with one another on the things that bring pleasure and the things that you do not enjoy. People often have questions about things like overcoming the negative effects of past sexual relationships, oral sex, frequency of sex, birth control, etc. There are a variety of Christian books written by experts on these subjects, and I would encourage you to get books from your local Christian bookstore, online or library to learn more about these topics.

෯**Nugget**෯ Finally, I want to address one other topic that has caused a great deal of pain in marriage, and that is impotency. I've talked to frustrated women whose sexual needs are going unmet because of their husband's inability to perform sexually. He feels like a failure and she is unfulfilled. There are so many dynamics involved that it's often embarrassing and difficult for both the husband and wife to talk about and work through. Thank God we live in a day and age where there are various treatments for these difficulties. I encourage you to be creative in your lovemaking approach and be sure to talk to your doctor about your options.

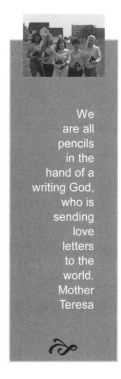

We are all pencils in the hand of a writing God, who is sending love letters to the world. Mother Teresa

The Fruit

Treating your husband well will enable him to be the best he can be. His confidence rises, he is satisfied with his wife and family, and he is able to fulfill God's plan for his life. Usually there are challenges along the way and it may seem that all of the "seeds" you are planting aren't producing much of a crop in your marriage or family, but if you will hold your position and continue to do good to your husband, you will see the fruit.

1.   Proverbs 31:23

        Underline the words "husband" and "he."

        Her husband is known in the [city's] gates, when he sits among the elders of the land . . . AMP

        If we will be the Christian, wife and mother God has called us to be, what are our husbands empowered to be in their vocation or sphere of influence?

        _____

2.   Proverbs 12:4

        Underline the phrase "worthy wife." Circle the phrase "other kind."

        A worthy wife is her husband's joy and crown; the other kind corrodes his strength and tears down everything he does. TLB

        What does a worthy wife give her husband? _____

        What does "the other kind" of wife do to her husband? _____

        How would you describe "the other kind"? _____

        You can make your husband feel like a happy king! Your Christian life and choices to be a godly wife and mom will crown his life and he'll be proud to have you by his side. If you are desperate for a great marriage, with God's help you can have one!

Scriptures To Chew On

Taking time to meditate on and memorize God's Word is invaluable. Hiding His Word in our hearts will strengthen us for the present and arm us for the future. Here are two verses to memorize and chew on this week. Write these verses on index cards and carry them with you this week. If you will post them in your bathroom, dashboard, desk, locker or other convenient places, you will find these Scriptures taking root in your heart.

> *"Wives, understand and support your husbands*
> *in ways that show your support for Christ.*
> *The husband provides leadership to his wife*
> *the way Christ does to his church,*
> *not by domineering but by cherishing."*
> *Ephesians 5:22-24, The Message*

> *"Marriage should be honored by all, and the marriage bed kept pure,*
> *for God will judge the adulterer and all the sexually immoral."*
> *Hebrews 13:4, NIV*

Group Discussion

1. Describe the importance of a Marriage of Three in your experience.

2. Describe the challenges married people face in our current culture as well as the work it takes to grow and maintain a marriage.

3. Which of your husband's needs do you need to be better at meeting and what is your strategy for improving?

---

[1]Schlessinger, Laura. The Proper Care And Feeding Of Husbands. New York: HarperCollins, 2004.

Personal Notes

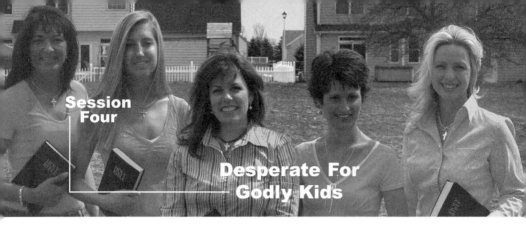

L ike a good new mother, I had every good intention of feeding my children healthy, balanced meals. But then, I regained consciousness. Why did I put myself through the torture? It would have been easier to prepare supper and then, rather than putting the food on the table for fifteen minutes while the kids picked at it and *then* throwing the food away, I could have just skipped the "table" step and thrown the food away right after I made it. But no, I played the game. You all know the game. *Food Threat. "You have to eat what is on your plate or else you will not be able to have a snack; you will go to bed early; you will never eat ice cream again in your entire life; and you will be grounded until you get married."* For some reason, when your child says, *"How many more bites do I have to eat?"* and then goes into the gag reflex, grandiose visions of being June Cleaver fly out the window. Can I get any amens? How many of you have lived this life?

Apparently, my work here is not done! Of course, I realized that when our oldest daughter, Meghan, was ten. *"Mommmmmmmm, Luke is bothering me. He just looked at me!"* Wow, what a crisis, so I ran to the rescue, *"Luke, tell Meghan you're sorry."* He rolled his 6-year-old eyes and said, *"Sorry,"* then burped in her face.

Then there's the trip to TJ Maxx . . . I was pregnant with our fourth child when I had a lapse in judgment and took three preschoolers shopping. Annie and Luke were in the shopping cart and Meghan was riding on the outside. I promised them ice cream if everyone behaved and obeyed mom. After all, I was eight months pregnant and just needed a few hours circulating with the real world, how

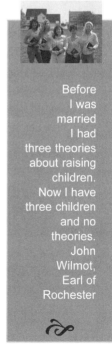

Before I was married I had three theories about raising children. Now I have three children and no theories.
John Wilmot, Earl of Rochester

crazy could it get? We'd been in the store for thirty seconds, when it began. *"Where's Meghan?"* I asked Luke, two and Annie, three and a half years old. *"Meghan, Meghan!"* I screamed in the store. *"Oh there you are hiding in the Misses rack. No, you don't need that bra yet, now stay on the cart, honey."* *"Annie and Luke, sit down, don't stand up in the cart."* *"No Annie, you can't have those work boots, let's put them back. Luke, let go of Annie's hair."* *"Meghan, get back on the cart, do you want ice cream?"* *"Sit down Annie. Don't lean, oh no . . . sit down I said, Annie and Luke don't lean . . . the cart is going to flip. . ."* That's when I became Hercules as I single-handedly gripped the flipping cart and flung it back into its upright position to ensure Meghan, Annie and Luke's safety and survival. It was also at that time that I became a transformer: nice mommy turned into raving wild woman. As I marched all three kids out of that store and to the car you could have heard my lecture three states away, *"I asked you to obey mommy in the store, didn't I? Don't you understand that I just needed a break today? I can't believe you kids acted just like 2, 3 and 5 year olds! We are not going to get ice cream, do you hear me? No ice cream for you! Blah, Blah, Blah . . ."* I am glad to report that the children aren't scarred, but we do have some funny memories! Of course, as a mother you have your own stories!

Raising kids is a joy and a challenge. As moms our heart longs for nothing more than to raise kids that turn out right—kids that love God, are obedient, kind and giving, joyful, successful, happily married and on and on. We want to raise kids that are unselfish and servanthearted; kids that feel worthwhile and valuable. We want them to be confident and articulate. It's our goal to help them become healthy and balanced spiritually, emotionally, mentally and physically. We train them up to leave and lead successful lives in God! We all know it doesn't happen by accident.

Let's look at the Proverbs 31 Woman and a few other verses of Scripture that encourage us as moms.

A Blessed Mom

1.   Proverbs 31:28

Underline the phrase "her children."

Her children rise up and call her blessed (happy, fortunate, and to be envied); and her husband boasts of and praises her . . . AMP

What do her children do? _____

When your children grow up, what would you like to hear them say?

_____

2.   Psalm 113:9

Underline the phrase "a joyful mother."

He maketh the barren woman to keep house, and to be a joyful mother of children. Praise ye the LORD. KJV

What type of mother will God make us? _____

How would you describe a joyful mother? _____

☙**Nugget**☙ Think about this. A happy mom—one that laughs easily, enjoys her children and is full of joy—what child wouldn't rise up and call her blessed? Sure, we have to discipline, set boundaries and train our children, but don't forget to be a joyful mother. When was the last time you goofed off with your kids? Stuck a French fry up your nose? Beat them in a burping contest? Played hide and seek?

What makes you and your children laugh? _____

_____

There are so many dynamics to motherhood—training children, disciplining, loving and nurturing, being an example, teaching the Word and more—but I want to focus on one of the most important roles we have as mothers, and that is the responsibility and privilege of praying for our kids. Let's talk about how to pray effective prayers that make a difference for our kids.

A Praying Mom

Abraham Lincoln said, *"I remember my mother's prayers and they have clung to me all my life."* Moms, your prayers make a difference!

If you ask most moms they will probably tell you they have prayed for their children, and yet they often live in fear, worry, doubt, anger and anxiety where their children are concerned. They worry about their protection. Their future. Their education. Their mates. Their friends. Their welfare. Their health. You name it. How can we pray in such a way that we know we have results? How can we pray effectively?

1.   James 5:16

        Underline the phrase "makes tremendous power available."

        . . . The earnest (heartfelt, continued) prayer of a righteous man makes tremendous power available [dynamic in its working]. AMP

        What three words describe the type of prayer that gets results?

        _____

        _____

        _____

        What does this type of prayer produce? _____

        ❧**Nugget**❧ I've heard people describe the phrase "makes tremendous power available" the same way we would describe making deposits and withdrawals. When we pray earnest, heartfelt and continued prayers for example, we are making tremendous power available; we are putting prayers on deposit so to speak. At the appropriate time, we make withdrawals and enjoy the dynamic workings of these prayers. A minister friend of mine says it this way: *"Prayer is the track we run on . . ."* In other words, as we pray we are laying down a spiritual track and making God's power available for ourselves and others—a track that we and they can run on.

2.   1 John 5:14-15

Underline the words "ask" and "hears." Circle the phrases "his will" and "we know."

14 This is the confidence we have in approaching God: that if we ask anything according to his will, he hears us. 15 And if we know that he hears us-whatever we ask-we know that we have what we asked of him. NIV

If we pray about anything according to His will, what do we know?

_____

If we know that He hears us, what do we know?

_____

How do you think you can know God's will?

_____

_____

His Word is His will. If we ask God on behalf of our children for anything according to His Word, then we can know He hears us, and if we know He hears us, we know that we have the thing we have asked Him.

Is prayer your steering wheel or your spare tire? Corrie Ten Boom

Ten Prayer Deposits To Make For Our Children

Effective prayer begins with knowing that what we are praying about is indeed God's will. If we find promises in His Word, then we know that is His will, and if we pray according to His Word, He hears us and grants our request. Praying earnest, heartfelt, continued prayers according to God's Word for our children will make tremendous power available for them. Our prayers will make tremendous deposits for their spiritual welfare. As we pray for our children, we are putting God's power on deposit for them to withdraw at the needed time. Isn't that amazing? Moms, our prayers make our kids rich in God!

What has God already promised us in His Word regarding our children? What prayers can we pray for our children, knowing that God hears us and that He will go to work on the behalf of our children? God's Word is loaded with promises He wants to fulfill. In prayer, we take God at His Word as we bring His promises to His very Throne and make our requests. Let's look at *"Ten Prayer Deposits To Make For Our Children."* After you've completed this section, I want to encourage you to use this as a guideline in praying for your children.

Deposit #1:
Pray For Your Child To Know Jesus Christ

1   John 3:16

Underline the promise to those who believe in Him.

For God so loved the world that he gave his one and only Son, that whoever believes in him shall not perish but have eternal life. NIV

Who can believe? _____

Whoever believes in Him shall gain what? _____

2.   Acts 2:38-39

Underline the phrase "to your children."

38 And Peter replied, "Each one of you must turn from sin, return to God, and be baptized in the name of Jesus Christ for the forgiveness of your sins; then you also shall receive this gift, the Holy Spirit. 39 For Christ promised him to each one of you who has been called by the Lord our God, and to your children and even to those in distant lands! TLB

The promise of forgiveness of sins and the gift of the Holy Spirit is available for whom?

_____

Deposit #2:
Pray For Your Child To Be Filled With God's Word

1.   2 Timothy 3:14-17

Underline "infancy."

14 But as for you, continue in what you have learned and have become convinced of, because you know those from whom you learned it, 15 and how from infancy you have known the holy Scriptures, which are able to make you wise for salvation through faith in Christ Jesus. 16 All Scripture is God-breathed and is useful for teaching, rebuking, correcting and training in righteousness, 17 so that the man of God may be thoroughly equipped for every good work. NIV

When did Timothy begin to learn the Word? _____

His mother and grandmother taught Timothy the Scriptures when he was just a baby and young child.

What does the Word do for our children? _____

What four things do the Scriptures provide?

_____

_____

_____

_____

2.   Psalm 119:10-16

Underline the words "commands," "word," "decrees," "laws," "statutes," "precepts" and "ways."

10 I seek you with all my heart; do not let me stray from your commands. 11 I have hidden your word in my heart that I might not sin against you. 12 Praise be to you, O LORD; teach me your decrees. 13 With my lips I recount all the laws that come from your mouth. 14 I rejoice in following your statutes as one rejoices in great riches. 15 I meditate on your precepts and consider your ways. 16 I delight in your decrees; I will not neglect your word. NIV

What can we pray for our children regarding God's Word? _____

_____

3.   Ephesians 1:15-19

Underline the phrases "remembering you in my prayers," "I keep asking" and "pray."

15 For this reason, ever since I heard about your faith in the Lord Jesus and your love for all the saints, 16 I have not stopped giving thanks for you, remembering you in my prayers. 17 I keep asking that the God of our Lord Jesus Christ, the glorious Father, may give you the Spirit of wisdom and revelation, so that you may know him better. 18 I pray also that the eyes of your heart may be enlightened in order that you may know the hope to which he has called you, the riches of his glorious inheritance in the saints, 19 and his incomparably great power for us who believe. NIV

What things did the Holy Spirit inspire the Apostle Paul to pray for those who believe?

How would you define the "Spirit of wisdom and revelation"? _____

How would you describe "the eyes of your heart" being enlightened?

In what way would this benefit your child?

∻**Nugget**∻ I remember a time when our third child, Luke, was really questioning his belief in God. One day he told me he wanted to see God and he didn't understand why God wouldn't just "appear" to him. We talked about it and I told him to read his Bible and see if the Lord spoke anything to his heart. A few days later, Luke told me that he was reading his Bible and he felt like God answered him when he read John 1:18 which says, *"No one has ever seen God. But his only Son, who is himself God, is near to the Father's*

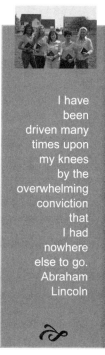

I have been driven many times upon my knees by the overwhelming conviction that I had nowhere else to go.
Abraham Lincoln

heart; he has told us about him." *NLT* God said more to my son in one verse of Scripture than I had said in twenty minutes. Although Luke didn't get to "see" God, he heard from God in a personal way through the Word. Helping our kids develop this type of relationship with God and His Word will serve them for their entire lives.

Deposit #3:
Pray That Your Child Would Be Led By The Spirit

1.   Romans 8:14

        Underline the phrase "led by the Spirit."

        For all who are led by the Spirit of God are children of God. NLT

        Who should lead us if we are children of God? _____

2.   Read 1 Samuel 3:1-10 for a great story on how children can hear God's voice and be led by Him.

Deposit #4:
Pray For Your Child To Live By Faith

1.   2 Timothy 1:5

        Underline the phrase "the faith of your mother."

        I know that you sincerely trust the Lord, for you have the faith of your mother, Eunice, and your grandmother, Lois. NLT

        Where did Timothy get his faith and trust in God? _____

_____

2.	Hebrews 11:6

	Underline the words "faith" and "believe."

	And without faith it is impossible to please God, because anyone who comes to him must believe that he exists and that he rewards those who earnestly seek him. NIV

	What pleases God? _____

	Whom does God reward? _____

Deposit #5:
Pray For Your Child's Personal Maturity

1.	Proverbs 22:6

	Underline the phrase "train up a child."

	Train up a child in the way he should go, and when he is old he will not depart from it. NKJV

	What is our responsibility as parents? _____

	If we do our part, what can we count on? _____

	_____

	I love this passage in the New Living Testament and The Message Bible translations:

	Teach your children to choose the right path, and when they are older, they will remain upon it. NLT

	Point your kids in the right direction—when they're old they won't be lost. The Message

You can pray for God's wisdom and grace to point your kids in the right direction and to help them choose the right path.

2.   1 Timothy 4:12

Underline the phrase "set an example."

Don't let anyone look down on you because you are young, but set an example for the believers in speech, in life, in love, in faith and purity.
NIV

In what ways can our children and teenagers set an example? _____

_____

_____

Since this is God's will, can we pray these things for our kids? _____

☞**Nugget**☜ God has wired each of our kids in a unique way. They have a God-given temperament, spiritual gifts and unique ways of communicating. When we try to fit our children into our cookie cutter mold of what we want them to be, we'll frustrate the grace God has given them to be the person He's created them to be. For example, if you have a son who's laid-back, creative, musically inclined and artistic, forcing him to be an athlete, all-star running back and the next CEO of your husband's company will frustrate the grace that God has given to him. Let's say you have a daughter that has been graced by God to be an outgoing, life of the party type of girl that loves playing basketball. If you want her to be quiet, organized and a frilly domestic princess, you will be disappointed and she will be frustrated. Let's discover the way God has wired our children and then cooperate with Him in nurturing those things and helping them to reach their greatest God-given potential.

Deposit #6:
Pray For Your Child's Education & Learning

Daniel 1:17, 20

Underline the phrase "God gave."

17 God gave these four young men an unusual aptitude for learning the literature and science of the time. And God gave Daniel special ability in understanding the meanings of visions and dreams . . . 20 In all matters requiring wisdom and balanced judgment, the king found the advice of these young men to be ten times better than that of all the magicians and enchanters in his entire kingdom. NLT

These four young men took a stand for God and the things of God. What did God give them?

_____

How much wiser were these four young men?

_____

Today, our kids need our prayers in their learning. With ADD, ADHD and other learning disabilities on the rise, let's seek the Lord on our child's behalf. We can pray that our children will live for God as Daniel did and we can trust Him to bless our children in their learning, as well.

Deposit #7:
Pray For Your Child's Friends & Mate

1.   1 Corinthians 15:33

        Underline the phrase "bad company."

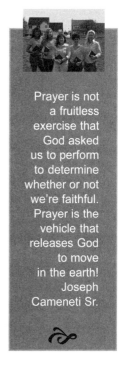

Prayer is not a fruitless exercise that God asked us to perform to determine whether or not we're faithful. Prayer is the vehicle that releases God to move in the earth!
Joseph Cameneti Sr.

Do not be misled: "Bad company corrupts good Character." NIV

What kind of friends will ruin your child's good character? _____

Pray for godly friends and divine, God-knit friendships for your kids.

2.	Proverbs 18:24

Underline the word "friends," "friendly" and "friend."

A man who has friends must himself be friendly, but there is a friend who sticks closer than a brother. NKJV

In order to have friends, what must we do? _____

_____

Pray for your child to be friendly, confident and outgoing in the realm of their comfort so that they make good friends.

Who's the friend that sticks closer than a brother? _____

Pray that Jesus would be their best friend.

3.	Mark 10:6-9

Underline the phrase "the two will become one flesh."

6 'But at the beginning of creation God 'made them male and female.' 7 'For this reason a man will leave his father and mother and be united to his wife, 8 and the two will become one flesh.' So they are no longer two, but one. 9 Therefore what God has joined together, let man not separate. NIV

What does verse 9 tell us? _____

Pray for God's best choice for your child's spouse. Pray that the Lord will order their steps to one another in His timing.

Deposit #8:
Pray For Your Child's Sexual Purity

1 Thessalonians 4:3-5

Underline the phrase "control your body."

3 God wants you to be holy, so you should keep clear of all sexual sin. 4 Then each of you will control your body and live in holiness and honor—5 not in lustful passion as the pagans do, in their ignorance of God and his ways. NLT

What does God want for our children and their sexual purity? _____

_____

↪**Nugget**↩ I am sure you are aware of the danger of Internet pornography for your children. Our culture is heavily sexual and the TV, music, movies, DVDs, Internet and often their friends are constantly trying to desensitize our kids to immorality, promiscuity, premarital sex, homosexuality, the party life and living on the edge. Our kids are truly being bombarded by sexual impurity! As parents, we have to be vigilant and wise in talking to our kids on these subjects. Moms, don't set the bar too low! Expect the best from your kids in purity, dating, dress and lifestyle choices. Impart God's values to them and pray that His Word and wisdom takes root in their hearts. There are many programs, books and tools available to us as parents and I encourage you to find those resources and share them with your kids at appropriate ages. I also encourage you to set some guidelines on what you allow in your home regarding music, DVDs, TV programs and Internet surfing. Let your kids know where the boundaries are and then stick to your guns and don't wimp out on enforcing them. You might want to check the "History" file on your computer to see where your kids have been browsing. It's in your child's best interest to help them live pure lives!

Deposit #9:
Pray For Your Child's Well Being & Long Life

1.   Ephesians 6:1-3

         Underline the phrase "first commandment with a promise."

         1 Children, obey your parents in the Lord, for this is right. 2 "Honor
         your father and mother"—which is the first commandment with a
         promise— 3 "that it may go well with you and that you may enjoy long
         life on the earth. NIV

         What two things are children commanded to do?

         _____   _____

         What two things does God promise?

         _____   _____

         Pray for the heart of your child to be submissive and obedient to you.
         Stand upon God's promise that life will go well for your child and God
         will grant them long life on the earth. We also ought to teach our
         children to respect all authority, governmental, civil, spiritual and
         educational leaders. We live in a society of disrespect, but as believers
         we ought to raise children that respect their parents, their elders and
         God-appointed authorities.

2.   Read Proverbs 3 for more insights on how to pray for your child's welfare
         and long life.

Deposit #10:
Pray For Your Child's Destiny & Future

1.   Jeremiah 29:11

Underline the word "plans."

For I know the plans I have for you," declares the LORD, "plans to prosper you and not to harm you, plans to give you hope and a future. NIV

What kind of plans does the Lord have for your child? _____

_____

Pray that your child will seek the Lord with his or her whole heart and find God and His will for their lives.

2.   Psalm 25:4-5

Underline the words "ways" and "paths."

4 Show me your ways, O LORD, teach me your paths; 5 guide me in your truth and teach me, for you are God my Savior, and my hope is in you all day long. NIV

What does God want to show your child? _____

_____

We can pray that God's plan, His divinely implanted sense of purpose and His ways, would be fulfilled in our children's lives. Ask God to open their hearts and spiritual eyes to desire and understand His destiny and purpose for their lives. Ask Him to order their steps. Let's pray and make prayer deposits for our children's futures.

Scriptures To Chew On

Taking time to meditate on and memorize God's Word is invaluable. Hiding His Word in our hearts will strengthen us for the present and arm us for the future. Here are two verses to memorize and chew on this week. Write these verses on index cards and carry them with you this week. If you will post them in your bathroom, dashboard, desk, locker or other convenient places, you will find these Scriptures taking root in your heart.

"Listen, my son, to your father's instruction
and do not forsake your mother's teaching."
Proverbs 1:8, NIV

"Therefore I tell you, whatever you ask for in prayer,
believe that you have received it, and it will be yours."
Mark 11:24, NIV

Group Discussion

1.　Describe some of the funny stories you've experienced with your kids.

2.　Which three of the Ten Prayer Deposits You Can Make For Your Children do you want to focus on for each of your children?

3.　Take time as a Small Group to pray for one another. Look to your left and pray for that mom and her children.

Desperate To Serve

When you think of great people, who comes to your mind? What qualities make them great in your thinking? Is it their Christianity? Is it their relationship with the Lord? Is it their character? Is it their accomplishments? Is it their influence? Is it their wealth? Is it their generosity? Kindness? Wisdom? What makes a person great in God's eyes?

One day several of Jesus' disciples were discussing this very thing. They were disputing among themselves as to who was the greatest among them. They were vying for the top spot on God's list! The most interesting thing is Jesus' response. He did not rebuke them for their desire to be great. He did not scold them for such an unrighteous desire. Rather, He defined greatness. His definition: Be the servant of all.

Me, Myself And I

We've become a consumer society where people expect to be served, rather than serve. Ask any church about the difficulty they have in recruiting children's ministry workers and you'll hear great excuses people use for "not serving." There is nothing more unbecoming than a self-absorbed woman. These days there are too many gals with the, *"Me, my and mine"* mantra. *"My life, my husband, my family, my money, my education, my job, my hobbies, my stuff. It's all about me!"* I hope this is not your story, but in the event it is, there is only one solution to this mentality—get over yourself! Serve. It's a sacrifice to serve. We have to say "no" to our wants. We have to rearrange our schedules. We have to sacrifice and give up some things,

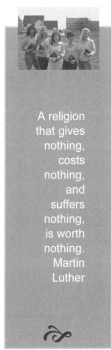

A religion that gives nothing, costs nothing, and suffers nothing, is worth nothing.
Martin Luther

trusting that if we do so with the right motives and for the right purpose, God will add whatever we need back into our lives. William Booth, the founder of the Salvation Army, in his final address to the army soldiers got up and simply said, *"Others."* With that, he sat down. Talk about making an impact!

If You Want To Be Great In God's Kingdom

Matthew 23:11-12

Underline the words "greatest" and "servant." Circle the words "exalts," "exalted," "humbled" and "humbles."

11 But he who is greatest among you shall be your servant. 12 And whoever exalts himself will be humbled, and he who humbles himself will be exalted. NKJV

To be the greatest in God's kingdom, what must we become?

_____

To be recognized as great in God's kingdom we must be humble servants of all.

Serve Your Family

The best place to start serving is in our families. My husband is the most servant-hearted person I know. He serves me and our kids in the most consistent and creative ways. He always seems to think ahead and he looks at the needs in our home and finds a way to serve. It's remarkable. Compared to him, I have room for improvement!

Let's look at the Proverbs 31 Woman to see how she did it.

1.   Proverbs 31:15

        Underline the phrase "she gets up."

She gets up before dawn to prepare breakfast for her household and plans the day's work for her servant girls. TLB

According to this verse, in what ways can we serve our family? _____

_____

It sounds like she gets up early! How many of you are early-riser girls?

What type of plan do you have for meals for your family? _____

_____

If you are like a lot of American families on the go, you find it hard to get everyone together for dinner on a regular basis. We have four children that are involved in sports and school activities, and at times it's a matrix challenge just to find a night everyone will be home to eat dinner.

Who does the Proverbs 31 woman plan the day's work for? _____

_____

I love that part of the verse! Can I get an Amen? She's talking about her domestic help—the cleaning lady, laundry lady and the cook. Life is good when you have help!

2.   Proverbs 31:22

Underline the phrase "she makes."

She makes coverings for her bed; she is clothed in fine linen and purple. NIV

Let's look at the Amplified Bible, as well.

She makes for herself coverlets, cushions, and rugs of tapestry. Her clothing is of linen, pure and fine, and of purple [such as that of which the clothing of the priests and the hallowed cloths of the temple were made]. AMP

What does she make? _____

It sounds like she is a talented seamstress and a great decorator. It sounds like she gives her bedroom a makeover on occasion and makes her home comfortable and homey.

In what ways could you serve your family through decorating and creating a warm environment for them?

_____

_____

❧**Nugget**❧ It's been said that "a man's home is his castle." We really do honor the Lord as we serve our family by keeping a clean, uncluttered, nicely decorated home. Have you taken a look around your home lately? Do the kids' bedrooms need a decorating update? Is your Master Bedroom a love nest for you and your spouse? There are so many creative ways to decorate on a shoestring budget these days, so why not set aside some time to update your décor?

3.   Proverbs 31:27

Underline the phrase "she watches."

She watches over the affairs of her household and does not eat the bread of idleness. NIV

What are we to watch over? _____

How would you describe "idleness"? _____

We can serve our families by acting as the "air traffic controller," keeping track of all the activities, domestic needs and affairs of our families.

Sleeping in until noon, watching TV all afternoon and then serving boxed macaroni and cheese for dinner is an example of an idle woman. God wants us to be actively serving our families.

In what ways can you improve in serving your family and watching over the affairs of your household?

_____

_____

Serve Others

1.   Proverbs 31:20

Underline the phrases "she opens" and "she reaches."

She opens her hand to the poor, yes, she reaches out her filled hands to the needy [whether in body, mind, or spirit]. AMP

Who does she open her hand to? _____

She looks for ways to help people with what types of needs?

_____

She is led by the Lord to seek out not just the poor in material goods, but also the poor spiritually, the poor mentally and the poor in body.

I don't know what your destiny will be, but one thing I know: the only ones among you who will be really happy are those who have sought and found a way to serve.
Albert Schweitzer

What are some practical ways you reach out to the "poor" (materially, financially, spiritually, mentally, physically) in your world?

_____

2.   Luke 4:18

Underline the phrases "to preach the gospel to the poor."

The Spirit of the LORD is upon Me, because He has anointed Me to preach the gospel to the poor; He has sent Me to heal the brokenhearted, to proclaim liberty to the captives and recovery of sight to the blind, to set at liberty those who are oppressed . . . NKJV

Who can we reach out to if we are filled with God's Spirit? _____

_____

Who in your sphere of influence fits these descriptions? _____

_____

3.   Proverbs 19:17

Underline the phrase "kind to the poor."

He who is kind to the poor lends to the LORD, and he will reward him for what he has done. NIV

If we are kind to the poor, how does the Lord measure this? _____

_____

What does God promise if we are kind to the poor? _____

_____

Serve In Your Local Church

Jesus is building His Church these days. If you want to be busy about the Father's business, get busy serving in your local church!

❧**Nugget**❧ I am a big advocate of serving God and serving others through your local church. Why not throw your hat in the ring and add your willingness to serve at your local church? The power of a local church in a community is immeasurable. The gospel is preached and families are ministered to through the local church. A local church full of servant-hearted people can absolutely influence a city for Jesus Christ. The local church facilitates outreaches to the needy, to prisoners and the poor in such a way as not only to "provide a fish," but to "teach people how to fish" so they get lasting help. The Church is front and center for Jesus! He said He would build His Church and the gates of hell would not prevail against it. I believe that every Christian ought to be serving families, the poor and their church community in some capacity through their local church.

We all have the same amount of time each day, each week and each month, and we must decide how much of our time we will sacrifice in service for God's glory. We all have unique, God-given gifts and talents which the Lord has given us so we can serve others. God has given each one of us a variety of things over which we are to be good stewards: over our life, our time, our talents, our material resources and our money. God is expecting us to use all of those things in our service to and for Him. In fact, a day of reckoning is on the horizon and the Lord will ask us to give an account of these very things. Let's look at this topic.

If you have personal issues with church, I want to suggest that you take it to the Lord in prayer. Usually, the reason people rebel against being involved in a local church is either because they also have pride or control issues; or are simply ignorant about the priority Jesus places on the local church. Jesus is the Head of the Church, and as the Great Shepherd of the sheep, He's focused on helping the undershepherds pastor the sheep in a local church while they reach out to a community to build His Church! If you are not part of a local church, with a God-ordained pastor, you are out of step with Jesus, the Head of the Church. I really encourage you to seek the Lord and His will in this matter. Let's look at this.

1.   Ephesians 4:11-13

Underline the phrase "to prepare God's people for works of service."

11 It was he who gave some to be apostles, some to be prophets, some to be evangelists, and some to be pastors and teachers, 12 to prepare God's people for works of service, so that the body of Christ may be built up 13 until we all reach unity in the faith and in the knowledge of the Son of God and become mature, attaining to the whole measure of the fullness of Christ. NIV

I love the way the Message Bible says this: *"He handed out gifts of apostle, prophet, evangelist, and pastor-teacher to train Christians in skilled servant work, working within Christ's body, the church, until we're all moving rhythmically and easily with each other, efficient and graceful in response to God's Son, fully mature adults, fully developed within and without, fully alive like Christ.*

Who called apostles, prophets, evangelists, pastors and teachers?

_____

According to this passage, what is the role of the apostle, prophet, evangelist, pastor and teacher?

_____

What does the phrase "to prepare God's people for works of service" mean to you?

_____

2.   1 Peter 4:10-11

Underline the phrase "use whatever gift he has received to serve."

10 Each one should use whatever gift he has received to serve others, faithfully administering God's grace in its various forms. 11 If anyone speaks, he should do it as one speaking the very words of God. If anyone serves, he should do it with the strength God provides, so that in all things God may be praised through Jesus Christ. To him be the glory and the power for ever and ever. Amen. NIV

Who has received gifts? _____

What are we to do with the gifts we have received? _____

Perhaps you wonder what gifts and talents He has given you. To help you evaluate your God-given gifts, answer the following questions and perhaps you'll be able to see a pattern revealing your giftings.

Your Thoughts: We often think about the areas we are called or gifted in. For example, those gifted in music think about music; writers think about writing, etc. What do you spend the majority of your time thinking about?

_____

Your Time: How do you spend your time? Your weekdays? Weekends? We usually spend time on the areas we are bent towards.

_____

Your Abilities: It's pretty obvious that many of your gifts or callings will be easy to recognize simply because you have a unique God-given giftedness, talent or ability in an area. What gifts, talents or abilities do you think the Lord has given you? What gifts, talents or abilities do others confirm that you have? Often, our friends see our

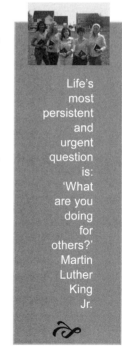

Life's most persistent and urgent question is: 'What are you doing for others?' Martin Luther King Jr.

gifts better than we do and if we are open, they can give us their honest appraisal.

_____

Your Service: What types of service do you lean toward? Serving children? Cooking? Teaching? Cleaning? Organizing? The way you desire to serve is a good indicator of how God has wired you.

_____

Your Money: The way we spend our money actually tells the real story. We do put our money where our mouth is. If we have a heart or calling toward world missions, that's where we put our money. If we have a heart or gift for reaching hurting people, we put our money into reaching the poor, hurting and needy. How do you spend your money?

_____

Your Relationships: How do you treat the people God has placed in your life? Are you energized or drained by people? Do you have a gift for relating to others?

_____

Your Body: Has God gifted you with physical abilities, athletic prowess or physical beauty? Are you using these things to serve God?

_____

There is a great sense of fulfillment when we serve God and others sacrificially. When we use the gifts and talents God has given us to serve our families and others, we are considered great in God's kingdom.

Scriptures To Chew On

Taking time to meditate on and memorize God's Word is invaluable. Hiding His Word in our hearts will strengthen us for the present and arm us for the future. Here are two verses to memorize and chew on this week. Write these verses on index cards and carry them with you this week. If you will post them in your bathroom, dashboard, desk, locker or other convenient places, you will find these Scriptures taking root in your heart.

> *"For you have been called to live in freedom —*
> *not freedom to satisfy your sinful nature,*
> *but freedom to serve one another in love."*
> *Galatians 5:13, NLT*

> *"Serve the LORD with gladness;*
> *Come before His presence with singing."*
> *Psalm 100:2, NKJV*

Group Discussion

1.   Describe some new ways that you can serve your husband and children.

2.   Describe the Biblical importance of serving in and through your local church.

3.   Describe the gifts and talents you believe God has given you for service.

Personal Notes

Desperate For Purpose

What on Earth are you on Earth for? Women want to know their purpose! It seems that the majority of the conversations I have with women these days have to do with these questions: *"What am I going to be when I grow up?"* *"What should I do with my life?"* *"What does God want me to do? When my children leave home, what should I do with my time?"* I believe *The Purpose-Driven Life* by Rick Warren has been a national best-selling book because people crave fulfillment of their purpose.[1]

When you really think about it, we are each allotted the space of several decades or so to live life, fulfill our destiny, potentially raise a family, leave a legacy, reach people for Christ and influence our world. Then, one day our "blip" will fall off the radar screen as we die and go into eternity. It's sobering, isn't it? Young girls dream about being wives, moms, nurses, teachers, doctors, LPGA players, movie stars, homecoming queens or even missionaries! High school and college-aged girls start asking questions about their purpose and destiny. Young career women and young moms are beginning to step into a part of their destiny. Those approaching midlife and an empty nest begin to give serious thought to the purpose, value and influence of their lives. Women in their twilight years reflect back and wonder if they fulfilled their destiny and they are either quite satisfied or full of regret.

As women, wives and moms, I believe we all want our influence to reach each member of our family in an eternal way. We want to be the authentic Christian God has called us to be. We want to love our husbands in a way that

A life isn't significant except for its impact on other lives.
Jackie Robinson

blesses him and honors the Lord. We want to raise kids that love God and want to follow His will for their lives. If we are successful in raising godly kids and sending them off to college, marriage or their own careers, we begin to think about the next phase of our lives and what God might have in store for us.

☙**Nugget**❧ Years ago, a woman I admire greatly shared this simple thought as I sat in her Bible class: *"Don't ask God to bless your plans. Find out what His plan is and follow it because His plan is already blessed!"* That's simple, isn't it? We don't have to strive and toil to come up with a plan and then pray that God will bless our plans. We just need to spend enough time in God's Word and in His Presence to hear from Him! If we will seek the Lord, recognize the season we are in, identify our God-given gifts, seek godly counsel and follow the Spirit, we'll fulfill our destiny. When we hear from God and know what His will and plan for the current season of our life is, then we can know without a doubt that His plan is already blessed. All we have to do is follow and obey. Isn't that a great thing to know? God's plan is already blessed; identify His plan and life is good. It takes all the pressure and mystery out of finding God's will. We don't invent it, we identify it! We follow it.

The Proverbs 31 woman seemed to have a good handle on knowing the season she was in and God's plan for her at that time. She recognized that God had given her exceptional entrepreneurial and business gifts, and as a result of following those things she maximized her life.

Let's look at this.

God Has A Plan For You

Are you ready for a life-changing journey? Will you be honest enough to ask and answer difficult, potentially life-changing questions? Can you handle an *"Excuse me; I interrupt your life to bring you this very important eternal destiny message . . ."*?

Here we go. Honestly, what are you living for? Are you living for yourself? Are you living for the approval or love of another person? Are you living for your kids? Are you living for the day you achieve some great goal? Are you living so you can die? Are you just living?

What motivates you to get up every day? What keeps you from being fatalistic? Depressed? Empty? Neurotic? Cynical? Disillusioned? Self-absorbed? Apathetic? Narcissistic? Sure, we all have responsibilities—marriage, family, work-related obligations and commitments to fulfill and take care of—but what really causes us to live; to live a life worth living?

The answer in one word: Destiny!

There is an "itch" inside all of us to fulfill our God-given purpose for being on Planet Earth. Have you tried to scratch that "itch" with busyness? With business? With family? With friends? With checklists? With planners? With e-mail? Internet and instant messages? With addictions? Achievements? Accomplishments? Accolades? With good works? Good ideas? Good intentions? Bet you've still got the itch, because until you "touch" your destiny, it's gonna itch!

༖**Nugget**༖ You do realize that you are on Earth for a purpose bigger than yourself, don't you? Don't live your life, take up space and breathe oxygen yet never fulfill your purpose for being here! Your destiny is bigger than just being married and having a family! As a wife, part of our purpose is not just to "be" good wives, but to pray and support and help our husbands be the men of God they are called to be. Don't let him settle for less. As a mom, part of our purpose is not just to "have" kids, but to raise up a mighty generation of kids for God! Don't let them settle for less! As a Christian, part of your destiny is to help Jesus build His Church—to influence those in your world for Christ by using the gifts, talents, time and wealth God has given to you. Can you see that your purpose is far bigger than giving birth, making sack lunches, cleaning house and watching your kids play basketball games?

Did you know the answer to the age-old questions, *"Why I am I here?"* and *"What's my purpose?"* is simple? Without sounding too cliché: *"You have a destiny!"* God has implanted a divine sense of purpose in the heart of every single person, and it's absolutely essential that you get intentional about identifying and fulfilling it!

The most fulfilled, satisfied person on the planet is the person who has discovered and is fulfilling their divine destiny. It doesn't get any better than that! I can honestly say that although I've made some mistakes in my life and there are some things I'd do differently if I had it to do over, I am confident that I am operating in the purpose for which I was created. I have been living in my destiny for the past 27 years; I don't doubt it for one minute. I know that I am living my life to please the Lord and that's all that really matters in the end. There is no better feeling.

The most miserable person on Earth is the person who has discovered their divine destiny, but is going 180 degrees in the opposite direction of fulfilling it! It's no wonder that celebrity after celebrity, rock star after rock star, athlete after athlete hits rock bottom and goes into rehab because they are using their God-given gifts doing things God never intended for them to do. They've missed their purpose. Thank God, He's merciful and the moment we repent and turn to God with a sincere heart, He extends His forgiveness and grace and we can get started fulfilling His purpose for our lives. Another very unsatisfied, empty, disillusioned person is the one who has not yet discovered their divine destiny, and therefore is not yet walking in it. Which person are you? You know your purpose and you're walking in it? You're running from God's plan for your life? You didn't even know God had a destiny for you, but you are interested in discovering it? Let's look at this subject.

1.   Ecclesiastes 3:11

      Underline the phrase "divinely implanted sense of a purpose."

      He has made everything beautiful in its time. He also has planted eternity in men's hearts and minds [a divinely implanted sense of a purpose working through the ages which nothing under the sun but God alone can satisfy] . . . AMP

      What has God planted into the heart and mind of each person? _____

      _____

      Eternity is defined as a "divinely _____

What can satisfy this sense of purpose? _____

Can anything but God and His plan satisfy you in the long run? _____

2.   Ecclesiastes 3:1

Underline the words "season" and "purpose."

To everything there is a season, a time for every purpose under heaven . . . NKJV

There is a season and a time for every what? _____

☙**Nugget**☙ It's important to discern the season of life you are in and discover God's purpose for it. For example, if you sense God's call on your life to preach the Gospel, there is a good chance that He will not lead you to fulfill that purpose in its fullness while you are a mother of preschoolers. This is because during the season of life when we have preschoolers, we need to be available for their needs and not traveling the world every week preaching the Gospel. Each person's life is unique and it's important that we prayerfully seek the Lord to understand the season of life we are in and discover His purpose for that time.

3.   Proverbs 19:21

Underline the words "plans in a man's heart" and "the Lord's purpose."

Many are the plans in a man's heart, but it is the LORD's purpose that prevails. NIV

What will prevail? _____

_____

Destiny is not a matter of chance, it is a matter of choice. It is not something to be wished for, it is something to be attained. William Jennings Bryan

Are you an idea person? Perhaps you have all kinds of ideas and plans for your life and maybe they just become a confusing blur in your mind. The thing to do is to get quiet enough to listen to your heart and see which "idea" persistently prevails and patiently waits in your heart. The Lord's purpose will prevail and continue to have a place within you. No matter how hard you try to erase it, God's purpose will not leave your heart. Often, it takes a season of getting quiet to discern it. Don't be in a hurry to "grab" at God's plan; be patient and let God settle it in your heart.

4.   Proverbs 16:3

Underline the phrase "His will."

Roll your works upon the Lord [commit and trust them wholly to Him; He will cause your thoughts to become agreeable to His will, and] so shall your plans be established and succeed. AMP

If we roll our works upon the Lord, what will He do? _____

_____

If your thoughts are not agreeable with or aware of God's will, then just make a decision to give Him every one of your ideas and thoughts and allow Him to work in your life.

∾**Nugget**∾ I remember a season my husband and I went through when we needed serious clarification on God's will for our lives. We thought we had been following the Lord's plan, but it was a rough season, so we spent some time seeking the Lord. We knelt by the couch and we imagined our heart was like a deck of cards—we saw ourselves laying out all the cards in our heart and presenting them to the Lord. Every thought, every idea, every desire—we laid them before the Lord and we told Him we'd quietly wait and allow Him to put the cards He wanted us to play with back into our hands. It took about 18 months, which required patience, but eventually the Lord let us know His will without question and we purposed to follow His plan with our whole heart.

Have you totally surrendered your life to the Lordship of Jesus Christ? Who's in the driver's seat of your heart—you or Him? Are you ready to follow Jesus, with an emphasis on "follow"? Let Him call the shots while you obey? There is no better decision you can make if you want to fulfill your God-given purpose.

5.   Psalm 32:8

Underline the words "guide" and "advise."

The LORD says, "I will guide you along the best pathway for your life. I will advise you and watch over you." NLT

What does God promise? _____

6.   Psalm 119:105

Underline the phrase "Your word."

Your word is a lamp to my feet and a light for my path. NIV

What does He say His Word will be for us? _____

The primary way God leads us and reveals His will to us is through His Word.

Maximizing Your Life

1.   Proverbs 31:13, 18, 24

Underline the phrase "her trading is profitable."

13 She selects wool and flax and works with eager hands . . . 18 She sees that her trading is profitable, and her lamp does not go out at night . . . 24 She makes linen garments and sells them, and supplies the merchants with sashes. NIV

In these verses, we can see that this Proverbs 31 woman is an astute businesswoman.

According to verse 13, what does she do with what is in her hands?

_____

According to verse 18, what has she learned about her business skills?

_____

Profit is good when you're in business. Have you ever had a job or business and discovered that once you paid your costs to work—childcare, gas, lunch and clothing—you really were not profitable?

According to verse 18, describe her work ethic. _____

According to verse 24, what type of business does she have? _____

The Proverbs 31 woman understands that her business skills are profitable and she is working hard. She knows what her talents and skills are and she is developing what she has!

&**Nugget**& I know several very successful, godly, profitable Christian businesswomen who are using their profession in the marketplace as their platform for serving and influencing others for Christ. It's awesome to see a balanced, on-fire, prosperous Christian businesswoman fulfill her purpose!

Unfortunately, there are many women that have been given gifts and talents and yet don't know what they have! They do not know what is in their hands, they do not know how to make a profit and they do not have the confidence necessary to give them the requisite strong work ethic. If that describes you, it's time you discovered that God has given you something that can be developed. God isn't too concerned with what you don't have; He is interested in what you *do* have! One of my favorite phrases in the Bible is, "*. . . what is that in your hand?*" That's exactly what God asked Moses one day. When the disciples were faced with the task of feeding over 5000 people, Jesus asked the disciples, *"How many loaves do you have?"* He didn't say, *"Wow, there sure are lot of people here and how in the world are we going to feed them? We just don't have enough, do we?"* No, Jesus simply asked—what do you have? He's still asking that question.

What do you have that you are willing to put into His hands? Your little bit in God's hands will be the base material for His miraculous purpose to be fulfilled. Let's look at a great story about a single mom with two sons and see how God turned this poor widow into a wealthy entrepreneur.

2.   2 Kings 4:1-6

Underline the phrase "what do you have in your house."

1 One day the wife of a man from the guild of prophets called out to Elisha, "Your servant my husband is dead. You well know what a good man he was, devoted to GOD. And now the man to whom he was in debt is on his way to collect by taking my two children as slaves." 2 Elisha said, "I wonder how I can be of help. Tell me, what do you have in your house?" "Nothing,"
she said. "Well, I do have a little oil." 3 "Here's what you do," said Elisha. "Go up and down the street and borrow jugs and bowls from all your

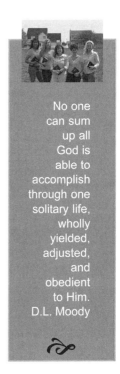

No one can sum up all God is able to accomplish through one solitary life, wholly yielded, adjusted, and obedient to Him.
D.L. Moody

neighbors. And not just a few—all you can get. 4 Then come home and lock the door behind you, you and your sons. Pour oil into each container; when each is full, set it aside." 5 She did what he said. She locked the door behind her and her sons; as they brought the containers to her, she filled them. 6 When all the jugs and bowls were full, she said to one of her sons, "Another jug, please." He said, "That's it. There are no more jugs." Then the oil stopped. 7 She went and told the story to the man of God. He said, "Go sell the oil and make good on your debts. Live, both you and your sons, on what's left." The Message

I love this story! It's the success story of a single mom that trusted God.

What was her lot in life, according to verse 1? _____

_____

This gal was a single mom with two sons and the creditors were coming to take her stuff. Ever been in a crisis and needed God's intervention?

In verse 2, what did the prophet Elisha ask her? _____

_____

How did she respond? _____

Notice that he wanted to help and he simply asked, "What do you have?" She was tempted to invite him to her pity party and she said, "Poor me, I don't have anything except this little 'ole jar of oil." I am sure she expected him to say, "You poor thing. Don't worry, I have a few million dollars lying around; let me take care of you." But he didn't.

What did he tell her to do in verses 3 and 4? _____

_____

It didn't look very supernatural, did it? In fact, it sounded like he asked her to work hard! He didn't want her sitting around moaning and groaning, but he wanted her up and using the little bit she had.

What did she do, according to verses 5 and 6? _____

Fortunately, she had enough faith to motivate herself and her boys to obey—they did what Elisha told them to do.

When it was all said and done, what did Elisha tell her to do in verse 7?

_____

By obeying God, this woman became the manufacturer, warehouse and distribution center, marketing and sales rep, and wealthy, debt-free CEO of her own oil business in one day!

This single mom became a CEO with two employees because she was obedient and gave God the little bit she had. He took it and touched it with His power! He multiplied her product until she had a garage full of oil inventory! Then, through her obedience to operate with a strong worth ethic and God's favor, she became the company's first marketing sales rep banging on doors to sell the oil.

God blessed her enough that she could easily pay her debts and get the creditors off her back, and with the money that was left over, she and her boys could live! Hello? Now that's a business God has blessed!

᠍᠍**Nugget**᠍᠍ Have you sought the Lord regarding your business? Are you doing what He's asked you to do and using the talents and skills He's given you? Has He given you any instructions that you have not obeyed? Do you believe He wants to touch and prosper your business? Are you willing to work hard, sell, market, provide services and do what it takes to succeed? When your business prospers, are you willing to be a good money manager and steward? Are you willing to use your wealth to help finance the proclamation of the Gospel as a debtor to those who need Christ? If so, God wants to help you!

As we conclude, let's look at the Proverbs 31 Woman one more time.

4.   Proverbs 31:16

Underline the phrases "she considers," "she buys" and "she plants."

She considers a [new] field before she buys or accepts it [expanding prudently and not courting neglect of her present duties by assuming other duties]; with her savings [of time and strength] she plants fruitful vines in her vineyard. AMP

This Proverbs 31 Woman is amazing! Not only does she have a great walk with God, a pleasing personality, an excellent marriage, wonderful kids, domestic skills, household help and a successful business, but she is a real estate mogul, too!

What does she consider? _____

What does she do after wise consideration, if she likes the piece of real estate she is looking at?

_____

Apparently, she has some discretionary income available for investment.

Is she flippant or hasty in her real estate ventures? _____

What does she do with the fields she purchases? _____

_____

She sounds like my mother. As a real estate agent for over 15 years, my mother was a pro at identifying profitable fixer-upper homes. Years ago, before it was as common as it is now, she'd purchase those homes through creative financing and fix them up with cosmetic and curb appeal. Then, she would sell them within a few short months to people needing their first home, often making as much as $20,000 on a sale. The buyer was thrilled and my mother was profitable!

꙰**Nugget**꙰ I'd like you to consider this passage from another angle. Have you ever considered the "fields" in your life? The field of your own spiritual life? The field of your husband? The fields of each of your children's hearts? The fields of the lives of particular friends, neighbors, co-workers and family members? Is there a famine in any of those lands? Are the fields barren and ready for some seed?

Once you consider these fields and determine that you need to give your attention to one or more of them, then plant a vineyard just as the Proverbs 31 Woman did! Begin to plant the seed of God's Word, of good deeds, or kind and faith-filled words into the lives of those fields. Water those seeds. Pray for those fields and watch God do some marvelous things!

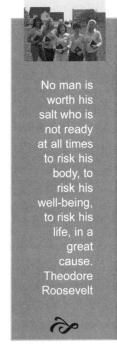

Satisfied lives for desperate housewives. Desperate for God. Desperate for balance. Desperate for a great marriage. Desperate for godly kids. Desperate to serve. Desperate to fulfill your purpose. It's my prayer that as you allow God's Word from these sessions renew your mind and get into your heart, you will find yourself knowing God more intimately and moving into the influential and satisfied life He has ordered for you.

By God's grace, we can follow in the footsteps of the Proverbs 31 Woman and perhaps one day we'll hear these things.

Her children rise up and call her blessed (happy, fortunate, and to be envied); and her husband boasts of and praises her, [saying], many daughters have done virtuously,

No man is worth his salt who is not ready at all times to risk his body, to risk his well-being, to risk his life, in a great cause.
Theodore Roosevelt

nobly, and well [with the strength of character that is steadfast in goodness],
but you excel them all. Charm and grace are deceptive,
and beauty is vain [because it is not lasting], but a woman who reverently and
worshipfully fears the Lord, she shall be praised! Give her of the fruit of her
hands, and let her own works praise her in the gates [of the city]! Proverbs
31:28-31, AMP

Let's close this Bite Sized Bible Study in prayer. *"Dear Father God, apart from
You I can't do anything. I come before You humbly and I ask You to help me to
be a doer of the things I have studied. I realize I need Your grace to stay hungry
for You, to find healthy balance, to enjoy a marriage made in heaven, to raise
a godly generation of kids for You, to use the gifts You've given me to serve
others and to fulfill the divinely implanted sense of purpose You've place inside
me. I ask for Your help in these things. Thank You, Lord, for helping me to be
the woman, wife and mother You have called me to be. In Jesus' Name.
Amen."*

Scriptures To Chew On

Taking time to meditate on and memorize God's Word is invaluable. Hiding His
Word in our hearts will strengthen us for the present and arm us for the future.
Here are two verses to memorize and chew on this week. Write these verses on
index cards and carry them with you this week. If you will post them in your
bathroom, dashboard, desk, locker or other convenient places, you will find these
Scriptures taking root in your heart.

*"I am able to do nothing from Myself [independently,
of My own accord—but only as I am taught by God and as I get His orders].
Even as I hear, I judge [I decide as I am bidden to decide.
As the voice comes to Me, so I give a decision],
and My judgment is right (just, righteous),
because I do not seek or consult My own will
[I have no desire to do what is pleasing to Myself, My own aim, My own
purpose] but only the will and pleasure of the Father Who sent Me."
John 5:30, AMP*

"May the God of peace,
who through the blood of the eternal covenant
brought back from the dead our Lord Jesus, that great Shepherd of the sheep,
equip you with everything good for doing his will,
and may he work in us what is pleasing to him,
through Jesus Christ, to whom be glory for ever and ever. Amen."
Hebrews 13:20-21, NIV

Group Discussion

1. Describe what you know and understand about God's plan, purpose and destiny for your life.

2. This may seem morbid, but if you had to write your own eulogy, what would you like to hear about the life you lived? Now's the time to make adjustments!

3. Describe what you "have in your hands" and how you intend to use this for God's purpose.

---

[1]Warren, Rick. The Purpose-Driven® Life. Grand Rapids: Zondervan, 2002.

The "Bite Sized Bible Study Series"
By Beth Jones

When your words came, I ate them;
they were my joy and my heart's delight . . .
Jeremiah 15:16 NIV

- Six practical Bible studies for Christians living in today's culture.
- Each book contains 6 sessions designed for individual & small group study.
- Great studies targeting men, women, believers and seekers of all ages.
- Convenient size 6" x 9", each book is between 80-144 pages.
- Fill-in-the-blank book with Group Discussion questions after each session.
- "Nuggets" throughout each study explain Scriptures in easy to follow way.
- Written in a contemporary style using practical illustrations.
- Perfect for small group curriculum, bookstores and churches.

Satisfied Lives For Desperate Housewives
God's Word On Proverbs 31
Great Study For Women, Retail $7.99
ISBN: 1-933433-04-3

Session 1: Desperate For God
Session 2: Desperate For Balance
Session 3: Desperate For A Great Marriage
Session 4: Desperate For Godly Kids
Session 5: Desperate To Serve
Session 6: Desperate For Purpose

Grace For The Pace
God's Word For Stressed & Overloaded Lives
Great Study For Men & Women, Retail $7.99
ISBN: 1-933433-02-7

Session 1: Escape From Hamsterville
Session 2: Help Is Here
Session 3: How Do You Spell Relief?
Session 4: Get A Bigger Frying Pan
Session 5: Houston, We Have A Problem!
Session 6: Time Keeps On Ticking

Call Or Go Online To Order:
800-596-0379
www.valleypresspublishers.com

Kissed Or Dissed

God's Word For Feeling Rejected & Overlooked
Great Study For Women, Retail $7.99
ISBN: 1-933433-01-9

Session 1: Dissed 101
Session 2: Blessed & Highly Favored
Session 3: Edit Your Life
Session 4: That's What I'm Talking About
Session 5: Sow Acceptance Seeds
Session 6: Just Like Jesus

What To Do When You Feel Blue

God's Word For Depression & Discouragement
Great Study For Men & Women, Retail $7.99
ISBN: 1-933433-00-0

Session 1: When The Sky Is Not Blue
Session 2: No Pity Parties Allowed
Session 3: The Things You Could Think
Session 4: Go To Your Happy Place
Session 5: You've Got To Have Friends
Session 6: Lift Up The Down

The Friends God Sends

God's Word On Friendship & Chick Chat
Great Study For Women, Retail $7.99
ISBN: 1-933433-05-1

Session 1: Friendship Realities
Session 2: The Friendship Workout
Session 3: God-Knit Friendships
Session 4: Who's On Your Boat?
Session 5: Anatomy of A Friendship Famine
Session 6: A Friend of God

Don't Factor Fear Here

God's Word For Overcoming Anxiety, Fear & Phobias
Great Study For Men & Women, Retail $7.99
ISBN: 1-933433-03-5

Session 1: Fear of Death
Session 2: Fear of Man
Session 3: Fear of Danger
Session 4: Fear of Change
Session 5: Fear Factors - Peace & Love
Session 6: Fear Factors - Faith & Courage

Why The Gory, Bloody Details?
By Beth Jones

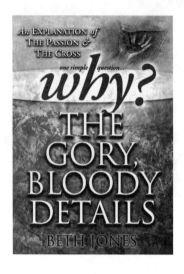

. . . right before your very eyes– Jesus Christ (the Messiah) was openly and graphically set forth and portrayed as crucified . . .
Galatians 3:1, AMP

Why The Gory, Bloody Details?
An Explanation of the Passion and the Cross

Retail Paperback $4.99, Hardcover $7.99

ISBN: 0-9717156-6-1 Paperback
ISBN: 0-9717156-7-X Hardcover

This contagious 96-page giftbook answers the basic question, "Why did Jesus have to die on the cross?" People want to know: Why did Jesus endure such brutality? Why did God allow His own Son to be murdered? Why the gore and blood? It's a great evangelistic gift for unsaved friends and family and a great educational resource for believers who want to understand the cross and the passion.

- *Evangelistic gift book explains the cross—perfect for seekers.*
- *Gospel presented in a relevant, easy to understand way.*
- *Gift book size 4" x 6", 96 pages.*
- *Written in a contemporary style using practical illustrations.*
- *Hardcover and paperback.*

A Ministry of Kalamazoo Valley Family Church
995 Romence Road
Portage, MI 49024
Ph. 800-596-0379
www.valleypresspublishers.com

Beth**Jones.org**

a

simple

casual

blog

articles

and

bible

studies

topics

like

eternal life

girl stuff

healing

ministry

finances

holy spirit

prayer

victory

faq

click

it

.